Trauma as Medicine

A DIY book for healing trauma and transforming your life

by Sarah Salter-Kelly

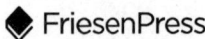
FriesenPress

Suite 300 - 990 Fort St
Victoria, BC, V8V 3K2
Canada

www.friesenpress.com

Copyright © 2021 by Sarah Salter-Kelly
First Edition — 2021

All rights reserved.

No part of this publication may be reproduced in any form, or by any means, electronic or mechanical, including photocopying, recording, or any information browsing, storage, or retrieval system, without permission in writing from FriesenPress.

Every attempt has been made to contact copyright holders. If copyright holders have not been properly acknowledged, please contact me, and I will be happy to rectify the omission in future printings of this book.

Authors note: This book is intended as a guide for spiritual healing. The approaches, exercises, ceremonies and tools listed herein are in no way intended as a substitute for medical care. It is to be utilized as an adjunct to the treatment received from a health care professional.

Order in bulk and save! Trauma focused organizations such as restorative justice, victim services, therapists, psychologists, church groups, spiritual centres, front line workers, mental health workers or book clubs contact me directly for a discount on purchases of 100 or more. info@sarahsalterkelly.com 1-780-314-9150 Follow Trauma as Medicine Facebook page or sarahsalterkelly on Instagram

ISBN
978-1-5255-9770-1 (Hardcover)
978-1-5255-9769-5 (Paperback)
978-1-5255-9771-8 (eBook)

1. Body, Mind & Spirit, Healing, Energy (Chi Kung, Reiki, Polarity)

Distributed to the trade by The Ingram Book Company

This book is truly a revelation. Through her living example, Sarah has demonstrated that nothing—truly nothing—is "too big" or "too hard" or "too anything" to fully heal and reconcile. If you are willing to go into this place of possibility with Sarah as your guide, this book can and will change your life.

–Maren Barros, M.Ed. aka Nahanni Dancing Coyote Woman
Teacher, Author, Speaker & Coach

By mindfully melding the personal and the professional of what shared humanity can mean when tragedy befalls us, Sarah Salter-Kelly offers hope, healing, and powerful medicine in this rich and thoughtful book.

–Margot Van Sluytman
Poet, Award-Winning Restorative Justice Researcher

I couldn't put it down! This book is a must-read for those struggling to rebuild or find purpose in their lives after suffering significant loss or trauma. *Trauma As Medicine* immediately yanks you from your seat and throws you into Sarah Salter Kelly's personal nightmare with gut-wrenching candor. Her subsequent quest for healing and answers becomes an alchemical journey that takes healing to a whole new level. The exercises, meditations, and ceremony included make *Trauma As Medicine* the perfect companion for seekers who are struggling to find their footing after immeasurable loss. Relatable and thought-provoking, *Trauma as Medicine* is not only a riveting true story of murder and forgiveness, it also sheds important light on the devastating ripple effects of colonization and residential schools in Canada.

–Marlene Chapman
Urban Mystic Consulting - Theurbanmystic.ca

Table of Contents

In memory of... vii
Forward ix
Dedication xi
Introduction 1

Part I: *The Trauma* 9
   Chapter 1: Blessing Our Journey 11
   Chapter 2: One Story of Trauma 15

Part II: *The Journey* 29
   Chapter 3: Approaching the Underworld 31
      Exercise: Intention setting 34
      Journal questions: Intention setting 36
      Journal questions: Spirit and Mother Earth 38
      Journal questions: Helping spirits and guides 41
      Journal questions: Ancestors 43
      Exercise: Connecting with a helping spirit 43
      Journal questions: Finding higher purpose 47
      Journal questions: Protection 49
      Journal questions: Showing up for yourself 50
      Journal questions: Getting into your body 53
      Exercise: Building an altar 54
      Journal questions: Setting up an altar 55
      Journal questions: Four directions 60
      Exercise: Place of power journey 66
      Exercise: Underworld journey 68
   Chapter 4: Tending to the Victim 73
      Journal questions: Addressing your victim self 79
      Journal questions: Reclaiming your power 82
      Exercise: Energy body #1 84
   Chapter 5: Why We Don't Feel and Why We Need To 87
      Journal questions: Feelings 94

  Exercise: Energy body #2 94
 Chapter 6: Intuition and Fear 99
  Journal questions: Instincts 102
  Journal questions: Triggers 107
  Journal questions: Projecting fear onto others 110
  Exercise: Energy body #3 111
  Exercise: Intuition #1 112
  Exercise: Intuition #2 113
  Exercise: Intuition #3 113
  Exercise: Intuition #4 114
 Chapter 7: Metabolizing Trauma 117
  Journal questions: Metabolization 128
  Ceremony: Addressing a person who has done you wrong 129
 Chapter 8: The Teachings of Forgiveness 133
  Journal questions: Forgiveness 138
  Ceremony: Forgiveness mandala 138
 Chapter 9: Ayahuasca and Trauma 141

Part III: *Gathering the Bones* 153
 Chapter 10: Finding Our Shared Humanity 155
  Journal questions: Collective healing 162
  Ceremony: Planting the seed of collective vision 162
 Chapter 11: The Colonial Wound 165
 Chapter 12: Healing with Marilyn, Peter's Sister 173
  Journal questions: Considering the bigger picture 178
 Chapter 13: The Sacred Hoop 179

Epilogue 183
Appendix: Tools for Ceremony 187
 Invocation of sacred space 189
 Offerings 195
Acknowledgments 197
Permissions 199
Resources, References and Next Steps 201
About the Author 203

In loving memory of my mother,
Sheila Salter
February 17th 1953 - December 7th 1995

Forward

I first met Sarah Salter-Kelly in a room flooded with fascinating people. Despite the competition, she stood out, a beacon of inner light. Her quiet warmth, strength, and presence appeared effortless, but she emanated something akin to a pulse that pumped something special, something *more*, into that space. I could tell she possessed enormous wisdom, but her humility offered no clue as to how she had acquired it.

But her wry humor was a dead giveaway to me.

After nearly 40 years as a therapist, I've come to recognize the source of such all-knowing wryness. I have only ever detected it in those rare individuals who have survived tragedy and managed to transform it into a powerful antidote to the events that wounded them. Sarah's dry, ironic, double-edged humor told me she was an alchemist of sorts. I knew her story would be one of transforming lived trauma into powerful medicine, and I knew I would benefit from hearing it.

The story you're about to read was a work in progress back then. Now you, too, can benefit from the wisdom of this extraordinary woman.

Sarah is what I call a *wisdom-carrier*. Her life has been a continuous journey of conscious revelation. She has earned a degree beyond anything an academic institution could grant; she is a master of lived experience. In the following pages, Sarah reveals her personal healing process and offers a crucial road map and compass. She guides you safely through the descent into the dark underworld of trauma and shares how to restore yourself to wholeness. She outlines steps to explore, heal, and integrate your own traumatic experience.

Sarah's need for healing came about following the tragic loss of her mother, Sheila. Sarah, just 20 at the time, idealized her mother as a strong, positive role model for herself, her family, and their community. Sheila was a spiritual teacher and a powerful proponent of New Age philosophy. She had an indelibly bright spirit and fervently believed that we create our own reality and that nothing happens without a reason. So when Sheila met an untimely and violent end, Sarah was saddled both with her mother's loss and with an excruciating and confusing mystery to solve. It was easy to see how Sheila's philosophy had shaped the way she had lived, but how could Sarah reconcile it with the horrendous way she had died?

I'll leave the answer that's revealed in the following pages in Sarah's capable hands, except to say that Sarah's courage, as a young seeker herself, is truly inspiring. I commend the passion with which she pursues the truth without candy-coating or white-washing her experience. Along the way, she comes to terms with herself while learning how to metabolize the darkness of murder, initiate the process of reconciliation, and make the decision to help others transform their lived traumas into medicine—a legacy of which her mother, were she here to appreciate it, would be incredibly proud.

Sarah's story takes you on a journey that will deliver balm to your soul. I consider it a must-read for anyone wrestling with trauma, and it should be on every therapist's recommended reading list.

–Gael McCool
Author of *Be Wise Now: A Guide to Conscious Living*

Dedication

This book is a love story.

For what better way to honour grief and trauma than tend to it?

What better way to consider forgiveness than embody it?

The deepest, most profound love of my life has come through meeting—inside my own body—the trauma of my mother's murder, and allowing myself to be with this most unspeakable horror, time and time again, as it broke me apart and transformed me.

The background of this tale bears the love of my husband, who has stood at my side for 26 years, held my tears, shared my joy, witnessed my storms, and always held space for my unfolding.

It is coloured with the texture of being a mother and the children who made me so— all of them—those that came through me and those who came to me. They turned me into the woman I am, graced me with humility, and blessed me with their love.

It holds the love I have for my mother, the love she had for me, shown and unshown, in this world and across the expanse to the next—the love that has only grown and deepened through the tragedy of her death.

Woven into its weft and warp are the cords of family and friends, whose belief in me and what I am sharing here has been immeasurable. In particular, my father's support, through all the moments he listened to me process over these past ten years, as I unearthed the trauma of my loss and surfaced my point of view— which at times contrasted with his—has been invaluable. I love you, Dad.

It is also a love story of shared humanity, and the love that rose up in me when compassion for my mother's perpetrator arrived (albeit uninvited) and I strove to understand and hold space for who he was and why he may have done what he did.

It is a love story for myself. A marker that says "Yes, I went here, yes, this is possible."

It is a love story for you. Yes, you can go there; yes, there is a way; yes, it is possible.

Let me show you how.

Introduction

Once upon a time, long, long ago—so long ago, in fact, that even the oldest of our Grandmothers' and Grandfathers' Grandmothers and Grandfathers cannot remember—there existed a time and a community that honoured and celebrated our deepest wounds as the passage of our soul's evolution. They knew that the initiation into higher learning came from fully embodying the energy of pain until it transformed into something inconceivable: something beyond the scope of the mind and into the wisdom of the soul. This was a process of allowing the poison of what had come to pass to rise up within, to care for this energy with wild dancing, music, crying, wailing, and other embodiment until it emerged as Medicine. It seems to me that these folks were in the long ago… but perhaps what I am imagining are the whispers of the ancestors yet to come: the ones who know that what the underworld has to teach us about who we are, and who we are becoming, is essential.

This is a book for those of you who are kin to these ancient future past ancestors—those of you who are tired of ingesting the poison of avoidance, denial, and spiritual bypass, and are ready to delve into the deep, dark territory of medicine-making.

This is a book for those of you who are hungry for more.

Making Meaning Out of Suffering

There is value and meaning in all that has transpired within our lives and on our planet. Discovering this meaning is up to each of us as individuals, and our willingness to do so is what opens the door to transforming trauma into medicine.

This book explores trauma from a spiritual perspective and draws on animistic philosophy, which recognizes an omnipotent force that organizes and animates the material world—one that is influenced by our relationship with it. It also works within the framework of pantheistic philosophy: the awareness that the universe is a manifestation of God/Spirit. These ideologies do two things: they empower us to recognize that we are on equal ground with the living universe/ecosystem of life, capable of tapping into this infinite force; and they reveal that we are not separate from anything. Most particularly, we are not separate from the stuff we don't like, such as our trauma.

I am going to use the word *underworld* to describe the territory we enter when we move into the energy of our trauma. This landscape is seen as the place we store the feelings we have not felt, the words we have not spoken, and the truths we have not claimed. We have a natural inclination to going there, whether conscious or not, because it holds what we know we are missing in our lives: the energetic domain of what is in need of transformation, be that unintegrated shadows, soul fragments, or unexpressed grief and trauma.

Living a rooted life, one connected to who we are and what has come to pass, asks that we have the courage to send our roots deep into our personal underworld territory and nourish ourselves from the heart of our greatest grief and trauma. The avoidance or denial of this poisons us. We cannot get grounded—rooted—without it, and the time we spend trying to ignore our pain leads to a surface experience of life. To live from the centre of our being, we need to go deep.

The underworld is an essential part of our human experience. Our navigation of it is emblematic of our ability to process and integrate our suffering. We have no power over the past, and when we live under the thumb of what has happened, we get stuck in a cycle of victimization and blame. Getting real means getting down and dirty with our own truth. What have we neglected, abandoned, or lost? What stories are we failing to tell? Who has hurt us? Who is haunting us? What power does fear hold over us? And most importantly, how may we use our trauma as a vehicle for transformation?

TRAUMA AS MEDICINE

How I got on this path

My understanding of the underworld has come to me through lived experiences and a personal drive for freedom. As I reflect on what has brought me to this moment in time, I can see that the seeds were sown when I was a girl.

I was born near the banks of the North Saskatchewan river, in the city of Edmonton, Alberta, on Treaty 6 territory. My ancestors came primarily from England, Scotland, Ireland, Germany and Russia. Some arrived a few hundred years ago and made their way north from the deep south of the United States; some traveled through Quebec and Ontario before their arrival on the prairies; and others still arrived in the last century. Many of them were homesteaders, seeking a better life for their family that wasn't possible under persecution or poverty in their motherland.

From a young age, I found my joy and shared my woes in the great outdoors. Perhaps it was the whispers of my ancestors that drew me outside, for I knew that the land held me. It was the keeper of my grief when I poured out my tears in my favourite grove of willows, lamenting the struggles with siblings, family, or schoolyard issues. It was the witness of my joy and freedom as I brought myself to the woods or the riverbank, time and time again, to sing my celebration of life. (Typically, this would include the old country ballads from Kenny Rogers, Dolly Parton or Juice Newton. "Angel of the Morning" still does it for me.) When I was outside, I was at home. I learned from a young age that the answers to my problems were found when I spent time alone in the natural world.

In my family, teaching religion and spirituality fell into my mother's hands. Though we were never baptized there were a few years where she went for a traditional approach, and I have many fond memories of Sunday school. As her search expanded into a New Age philosophy our times at church ended and were replaced by more encouragement to talk to God myself. As a teen, I was enrolled in personal growth and self-help workshops that fostered a deep faith in my ability to be myself and create what I want.

I was innately curious about ways to pray, particularly in nature. Living in close relationship to the ancestors of the land now, I know they were guiding me back then. They had been stewards of that area for thousands of years, and it was their voices that drew me. I was also pulled by the ancestors of my bloodline, and it was in seeking out my pagan roots that I discovered Wicca (specifically, the Reclaiming tradition) at age sixteen. The novelty that there was such a thing as real witches who were good was awe-inspiring, particularly seeing female archetypes in positions of sacred power. For many years, I was a devout and committed Pagan. On a full-moon solstice night in my seventeenth summer, I created my first ceremony, declaring my life-long service to the Goddess out loud, bare feet on the earth, the promise of my commitment filling every fibre of my being with its power.

My Pagan practice deepened through community ritual, workshops, and personal experience until I was 30. This background was instrumental in fostering a healthy relationship with the energetics of spirit: connecting energetically to the trees, the animals, the land, the rivers (to name a few), as well as my own spirit guides, power animals, and ancestors. I felt at home in the Reclaiming tradition, as it was all-inclusive, and its principles encouraged me to develop my skills in creating ceremony and ritual. In hindsight, I see these teachings as the integral structure that held me when my mother was murdered and I needed a means to be with my grief and address my trauma. Once again, I was outside in the woods, singing or creating my own rituals to release my grief. In Paganism, moving into the underworld is seen as a natural part of the wheel of the year, like the seasons of fall and winter. There are infinite myths to pull from, like the descent of the Sun God between solstices, or the journeys of Demeter and Inanna into the underworld, and of course the subsequent gifts of their passage inwards.

Around the age of 30, I went through an intense process of sitting in the underworld with the spirit of my mother's perpetrator for close to a year—a ceremony and process that is documented in this book and was instrumental in its creation. This formalized my calling to shamanism.

Following this experience, I sought out human teachers in shamanism. This search led me to Peru on eight different occasions to study the teachings of the Q'ero Nation, starting in 2008. They are renowned energy healers living high in the Andes, whose culture and spiritual teachings remained intact at the onset of colonization due to their remote location. One of their elders, Don Manuel Quispe, began teaching westerners before the turn of the millennium, and many of his people followed suit. The gifts of this lineage are finely integrated into the teachings in this book. I spent time in the Amazon as well, working with Grandmother Ayahuasca, and I have included those discoveries in Chapter 9. One of my favourite American teachers is Nicki Scully, who teaches Alchemical

Healing and Egyptian mysteries. Her focus on teaching people to journey for themselves was instrumental in my understanding of shamanic *journeying*, and the integration of this technique in my private practice. There were numerous other teachers, techniques, and courses that supported my understanding of trauma, my place in it, and the natural world around me. These varied from restorative justice courses (such as Peace Circle Facilitation and S.T.A.R. Level 1 - Strategies for Trauma Awareness and Resilience), holistic health (such as herbal medicine, plant spirit medicine, and aromatherapy), energy healing (including Reiki Master Teacher), and Yoga (yin).

I am also mother to three children with my husband of twenty one years and have two stepdaughters through him. I feel like motherhood and healthy partnership are cardinal teachers whose influence cannot be minimized. These people are my gurus, and they show me daily how I can open to being a better human.

Since 2007, I have had a private practice in energy healing and shamanism that has included facilitating anything from weekly circles and retreats to a two-year integrated program for Shamanic Practitioners. I started teaching Trauma as Medicine weekend retreats in 2013 and by the time of this book's publication, there will also be "Trauma as Medicine" courses online to help implement its teachings.

Over the past ten years, I have shared this story at many conferences throughout Alberta. Since 2015, I have done so alongside the sister of the person who killed my mother (yes, that, too, is discussed in this book). Writing this book is the natural outcome of my journey since my mother's homicide in 1995.

My expertise in transforming trauma into medicine comes from personal experience, practice, observation, witnessing clients, and teaching students through the years. I am, first and foremost, human, and subject to the weakness of seeing things through the blinders of my own perspective. Therefore, my approach to trauma may or may not be a fit for you. On your own healing journey, please get proper medical and psychological support as needed.

The path of this book

My intention in sharing this story is to offer resources to guide you in the healing of your own trauma. My personal experiences are integrated into the text, depicting real-life examples to give context to the content. I am a storyteller, and I believe it is through stories that we heal.

In Part I, I take you into the experience of my mother's homicide and trial to give you a visceral representation of the underworld through story. It is my hope that sharing these intensely painful and emotional events will help you to foster courage in facing your own trauma.

In Part II, I discuss the following concepts, including ceremonies and practices to support your journey. Each of these elements instigates the reclaiming of your power and actions required to make medicine through moving deeper into your own grief or trauma.

- Approaching the underworld
- Tending the victim
- Expressing the feelings
- Intuition and fear
- Metabolizing trauma
- Forgiveness and teachings

These components are fundamental. Though I offer them in structure, note that our healing rarely is; many of these steps will occur out of order, at the same time, backwards, and more than once. What this list does illicit is the awareness that each of these elements will most likely show up at some point along the way.

Also included in this portion is a chapter on Ayahuasca. For those who feel called to exploring her medicine for addressing trauma, addiction, or health issues, there is helpful information for you, including stories from my own experiences in the Amazon, and an interview with the Ayahuascero I worked with on five separate occasions.

In Part III, the focus broadens to a collective point of view, as I inquire deeper into my own story and contemplate a shared humanity with my mother's perpetrator. This culminates in a journey of exploring and investigating what transpired to set him on this path, and includes my take on our collective responsibility to healing trauma. Here I go into the history of colonization in Canada, my understanding of how white privilege and institutional racism influenced my mother's death, and what has motivated me to educate people about Canada's historical and present-day reality for First Nations (to the best of my ability).

There are also journal questions, exercises, and ceremonies in this portion, to jumpstart those who are called to collective medicine-making.

Essential concepts for this book

A few terms I use throughout this book may be unfamiliar to you, or you might see them in a different way. To make sure we are on the same page, I'd like to give you my definitions of them here.

Healing. The act of bringing love, attention, and awareness to what is out of balance within us. It is not a destination we reach where all of our soul work is completed. Like the turning of the wheel of the year, we revisit our wounds in cycles. Healing is the ability to be conscious, present, and consistent in caring for ourselves with love and kindness.

Medicine. The art of creating an energetic elixir from your soul wounds. Medicine generates gifts that enhance your evolution and understanding of who you are.

Soul wounds. Experiences from this life or another—typically grief or trauma that mark you in such a way that you do not feel free to be yourself or open to the light of possibility within.

Felt sense. The engagement of all five senses plus your sense of knowing. An embodied experience of perception.

Earth as Mother/Mother Earth/Pachamama. The spirit of the Great Mother, who holds us, loves us, and nurtures us through the physical manifestation of this world we live on with all the abundance she provides.

Spirit. God, Universe, Creator, Great Spirit, Father, Son, Holy Spirit, You who are known by a million names and You who are the nameless one, Great Mystery.

Spirit is the term I use to describe the omnipotent, miraculous life force that connects us all. It is my belief that each of us bears an element of this divinity within us. Spirit with a capital "S" is the macro; the micro-spirit, we have within, and everything is sourced from this one life force. Please feel free to substitute the word that feels right for you.

Shaman or Shamanism. A shaman is a person whose relationship with Spirit enables them to navigate the dark (think suffering, trauma or grief), understand the energetics of existence, and in turn use their skill, consciousness and ability to bring about balance. Shamanism is the practice of this concept, a lifestyle that focuses on the reciprocal relationship with self and the ALL, which often includes ceremony, prayer, shamanic journey and service.

* * *

My intent

What if our suffering and how we address it holds the keys to our personal and collective awakening?

I believe it does. I believe we are the resources that we seek. Often we dress up the expert in the clothes of another and cannot see the value inherent in our own being—the value that shows up when we slow down and listen to what our souls are asking of us.

We become empowered when we embrace ourselves for who we are and stop seeking external references to define our worth. This empowerment is found through the healing of our trauma, honing in on our capacity to navigate the dark. I hope that sharing my story will inspire you to dig deep and be the alchemist in creating your own soul medicine.

PART I:

The Trauma

CHAPTER 1:
Blessing Our Journey

> Take three deep and cleansing breaths into your heart centre.
>
> See if you can deepen it with each intentional inhale and exhale.
>
> Inhale and exhale…
>
> … so that breath by breath, you are connected to what is here.
>
> Breath by breath, you are here.
>
> Breath by breath, you are present.
>
> Close your eyes, if you have not done so already, and move fully into your heart space.
>
> And so we begin.

I acknowledge that the events recounted in this book took place in Treaty 6 territory of Alberta, Canada.

* * *

I call in your ancestors and I call in mine.

Grandmothers and Grandfathers, we honour you: those who have gone before us, those who are here now, and those who are yet to come. Those who breathed us into being and those who we are breathing now, welcome.

Ancient ones, I beseech you to encircle us with your wisdom. Help us find the courage necessary to tend the needs of our soul.

May this soul work be our priority. May we choose ourselves and our healing over the need to please others.

May we choose ourselves—our authentic, wild, and soul-felt selves, and our fractured and broken selves—and through this choice, may it be known that we name ourselves as whole and worthy.

Guide us through the fires of adversity and conflict in such a way that we are strengthened. Help us to be with our greatest fears so they no longer have the power to bind us, and teach us to listen to our gut instinct.

I welcome in our helping spirits—yours and mine, known and unknown...

Protectors, allies, and guides; power animals, angelic ones, and mythical beings, be with us. Open our vision to the multifaceted perspective you are here to share with us. Help us feel safe in being vulnerable, get out of our heads, and awaken to our profound connection with all of our relations. May this awakening change us.

Gathering this prayer up, we move it through the midline of our bodies down through our legs and root chakras, so we are grounded in the medicine of the Mother Earth below us. Sending our roots out in every direction simultaneously, we are anchored and connected to all that is needed to feed our body, mind, and spirit.

Great Mother, by all the names in which we know you, I welcome you intentionally into this space. Support us in stopping and listening while this story is told. Help each person tune into what they must hear to support their own healing journey, leave what is not necessary for them, and share what is in support of the healing of all beings. Help each reader identify and acknowledge their own unresolved suffering without measuring or comparing, and in turn foster the nourishment needed to heal.

Also, Great Mother, I am going to speak of heinous acts of violence against a woman—my mother—and I need help creating a container to hold this. May this be solid and strong and may the telling of this tale support women and family members of women who have been impacted by abuse and violence.

Gathering this prayer, we breathe it up through our body. It moves up the midline of our spines and extends out our crown chakra as if we are the Tree of Life itself, with our branches moving out in every direction simultaneously, touching all that is above.

Great Mystery, by all the names in which we know you—God, Goddess, Creator, Great Spirit, Source—I welcome you into this space. May Grace be the power that motivates and inspires what is written and what is read. May we each touch the Divine light within ourselves and realize the truth of who we are. May this touching of the sacred galvanize what we see, what we hear, and what we do. Open each of us to the infinite possibilities of this moment.

Also, Great Spirit, I am going to share stories of the degrading acts committed in the name of colonialism, white supremacy, institutional racism, and misused power. Please help create a container that may not only hold this, but transform it. Allow the telling of this tale to weave its energy in support of shared humanity and reconciliation.

Breath by breath, Inhale by exhale, In service to all of our relations, May it be so.

Sarah Salter-Kelly
White Raven Woman
Winter Solstice 2019

CHAPTER 2:
One Story of Trauma

Sharing our stories

This is the formal marking of my descent into the underworld. Telling my story lays the foreground and context for our journey together in this book. Our stories are the vehicles that open us to understanding who we are. Through their telling, time and time again, we heal.

Murdered

The day my life changed forever was the seventh of December, 1995. I had just turned twenty years old. On this day, one story ended and another began.

It feels like only yesterday as time and space shift and change in the face of trauma. Suddenly, something so solid and reliable becomes stretched like an elastic band, and instantly, one day, one month, and even one year holds more detail than any other remembered.

The mind holds on to these details, because when all else is falling apart, the details themselves define the landscape. Those details bring form to the formless and sense to the senseless. One feels that if enough of them are collected and stored, they will somehow give direction to navigating the foreign territory of trauma.

I can recall the sound of each news station before the journalist spoke—that few-second lead that announced an update—my focus riveted to the screen in anticipation of maybe *finding out what happened,* then the long pauses as I waited and waited. I remember the detail of the word *missing* hanging in the air like a lead weight, alongside *mother of three* and *police are searching.* Not to mention the sensation in the room as I sat with my family on that first day and witnessed how each of us was impacted by the news, each person's despair and helplessness a mirror for my own.

In some way, the cold was the worst detail of it all, maybe because of how much Mom hated it. There was a sharp cutting sensation of air in my lungs when I went to work that morning, with the thermostat at -38 Celsius... even though, at that moment, I didn't know yet. Even though I had yet to imagine her, as I would in the days to come, outside somewhere in the cold. Frozen.

It was only afterwards that I thought of the connection: how hard it was to breathe, as if the cold was choking me on my short walks from building to car, car to building. I chalked it up to a normal response to the inclement weather. The truth is, the cold does something to a person. In the northern city of Edmonton, Alberta, we pretend we are okay with it at the initial onset of winter. We even laugh about our fortitude. But when it drops below minus thirty centigrade, there is a change, a palpable shift in the breathless air, the breathless people, as if we are all holding our breath, afraid of what might happen if we exhale.

It is in winter, after all, that we come face to face with the dark side. Enhanced by the waning hours of light and freezing temperatures, a space is revealed where we must reckon with our own fears. Generally, we do not anticipate that those fears will be met.

As I write this twenty-five years later, I still can't soften the blow of this story. It is not soft. It is cold like the air was the day that everything changed. It is cutting, and it is painful. Even now, it is shocking to me as I write it, and to you as you read it; this is simply the truth of violence.

Shortly after 8:15 a.m. on that winter morning, my mother, Sheila Salter, was abducted by a stranger from the ground-level parkade of her workplace. She was raped and murdered. Her body was taken out of town and tossed into an abandoned farmhouse, remaining undiscovered for ten days.

When I look back at that time, the memory brings the physical sensation of pressure in my belly. Every piece of traumatic information I absorbed landed smack dab in the centre of my gut: the fact that she had not arrived in her office that day, but that someone had found her glove and briefcase, or the fact that a program participant had waved at her only a few minutes short of her assumed arrival. This pressure built with each detail I consumed over the days to come: the blood found in her truck, the earring on the floor of the parkade, the words from the news headlines—*Abducted* and *Cops Search for Body*; then, a few days later, *Police Call Off Search*.

I struggled to relate every piece of information to the mother I loved and treasured. I recall pushing the word *abducted* around in my mouth with my tongue, saying it silently to myself, saying it out loud, realizing it led to a series of end results I did not want to fathom. I did not want to swallow this word. But it landed with the rest of the details in my core, sitting undigested as the clock ticked by and I waited.

Missing

Mom was missing for ten days. For ten long days, we did not know what had happened to her. When your family member has been abducted, much of the trauma lies in having no control over the present circumstances, and your fear of what the unknown outcome might entail. The state of *missing* is impossible to be in. The body is in a constant trauma response, the mind searching for and listing the "what ifs" of the worst-case scenarios. I was concerned that thinking about them at all might draw them near, but I was not always able to monitor the direction of my mind. How to live in this space of no control? What do you do when you are faced with this reality? I hoped. For her sake, I hoped. I prayed my ass off. At night, I would visualize her in a safe space, her head resting on my lap, my hands holding her crown chakra as I sent her all the love I had. I talked to her non-stop, telling her how much I loved her. This gave me the sense that I could do something—even if it was this small—and that maybe this act would help generate the outcome I wanted, the one where she was found alive.

The experience of shock is heightened by the confusion of trying to reconcile what *is* happening with the expectation of what *should* be happening. There is no map; just the accumulation of details and the ability to get through each second, minute, maybe even hour. How surreal it felt to see my mother on the front-page news stories—my *mother*—now symbolizing every woman's greatest fear: to be accosted by a stranger in a dark place and disappear. All I could think was,

"This can't be happening." Surely, at some point, my mom would come waltzing in and say "Ta da! Just kidding." I remember sitting in my kitchen on day two of *missing,* taking a mental inventory of normalcy. Clock ticking on wall, check; cats meowing to be fed, check; neighbour going to work on time, check; plant needs to be watered, check; mom at work where I can call her—no check. How could so much be normal when that one fact made everything else fall apart? Why did the world around me look the same when nothing felt the same on the inside?

Reality as I knew it came crashing down. I was, like my mother, a devout spiritual seeker. I had the naiveté to assume that being on a spiritual path accredited oneself a level of protection—that Spirit would take care of us because we worked in service to the whole. I felt like my mother had been forsaken. That I, we—my family—had been forsaken. On the third day that she was missing, Mom was supposed to have left on a two-week spiritual retreat with her mentor, Shakti Gawain, in Hawaii. It would have been the first time she'd ever done anything like that for herself. How could something like this be happening to her now?

The night she went missing, her vehicle was found with a pool of blood in the back and other viable DNA lifted from the steering wheel and interior. I asked a police officer directly how much blood was found, hoping and holding on to the idea that she might be okay. Bless him for wanting to protect me when he said the blood could have been from losing a finger. God, I held on to that notion with some level of solace over the days to come. Even if it was false hope, at the time it helped. Sometimes we need that.

In the undercarriage of the car's wheel wells there was wild grass, indicating it had been off-road, but so much snow fell in the next few days that the trail went cold. The police had to call off the search by day three, and they appealed to the family as well as the citizens of Edmonton for any information that could possibly be of help. People were asked to search their garages, yards, alley ways, and outbuildings.

Everyone in my family, intimate and extended, racked our brains for something that could somehow be helpful to the investigation. Anyone we knew who had had even the most minor transgression or potential negative thought towards Mom became suspect on our list. Rarely, our detective had told us, was homicide committed by a stranger. I recall a family meeting where my aunts and

I discussed for hours on end who it could possibly be, and then my own fear as the minutes ticked by, that somehow we would not name the right one, and we would lose her because of our failure to do so.

There was something unique about the impact her spirit had on the city of Edmonton. Even today, nearly twenty-five years later, people remember Sheila Salter. Much of this was due to my family sharing anecdotes and personal stories at the press conference, so that she remained a real person and not an object. We knew that if she was objectified, we would be less likely to find her. It is so easy in general to desensitize oneself to what is heard in the news. To keep people sensitive, interested, and helpful to the investigation we shared personal stories from our hearts. And it worked. Droves of volunteers helped look for her, people offered potential details, and every resource the city had was put towards finding her. Friends and strangers set up tables in malls busy with Christmas shoppers to sell white ribbons, a symbol to end violence against women. The money was donated to local shelters. In spite of the trauma, in spite of not knowing if she was dead or alive, I could feel my mother's spirit at work.

* * *

Sheila Maureen (Miseck) Salter was a daughter of the Peace Country of northern Alberta. She was born in the Eaglesham stationmaster's house in February of 1953. Her father worked for the Northern Alberta Railroad, and her mother was, at the time, a stay-at-home mom. She met my father at eighteen; they married a year later, in 1972, and had three children. Mom was fuelled by her spiritual path, and became more committed to it when she lost her sister suddenly to pneumonia around 1985. She brought everything she learned to the kitchen table to share, which meant that the philosophies of Louise Hay (*You Can Heal Your Body*) and Shakti Gawain (*Creative Visualization*) became staples in our home. She trained as a life skills coach (what is now known as a life coach) and eventually started her own business, which was housed in the building she entered for the last time on that fateful December morning. Her faith in the creative potential of our spirit and our universe had a profound effect on me. She was my first spiritual teacher.

Found

It was my aunt who remembered her one-of-a-kind ring, a ring my Dad had had made for her a few years prior as a last-minute Christmas present. When we held a press conference, we had a copy of this ring made by the original jeweller to share with the general public, and it ended up being the piece of evidence that linked us to a potential bad guy.

The owner of an inner-city hotel had purchased the ring around noon on December seventh, from a man by the name of Peter John Brighteyes. A Canada-wide warrant was issued for his arrest.

I recall my maternal grandfather being so upset when he recounted that "Brighteyes" was the nickname he had called my mother when she was a girl.

On December eighteenth, a farmer near Chipman, Alberta headed out to an abandoned farmhouse on his land to bring in an old wood stove. When he entered the building, he discovered my mother's partially-clad body frozen to the floor. She had been tossed in through a window.

* * *

There was definitely relief in knowing what happened to her, but the relief was short-lived in the face of *what happened to her*. I remember being at my aunt's house when I heard the news. I stood up, calmly walked over to the bathroom, and threw up the solid mass of energy that the details had formed in my belly over the past eleven days.

Now we as a family could do the things that were necessary to say goodbye—once her body defrosted and a full autopsy was performed. This is one of the gruesome realities of homicide.

Three days later, Brighteyes turned himself in, wearing running shoes stained with the blood of my mother, and pled *not guilty*. I had watched the news and read the stories that appeared about him. He had been in the system since childhood and was a violent offender. He was Cree, from Saddle First Nation. One week prior to my mother's death, he had been released from the Aboriginal

Treatment Centre, where he was incarcerated. His Elder had said he was healed and ready to integrate into society. There was so much wrong with this picture.

I can't say I was happy we found the bad guy. It just doesn't work that way with murder. There was perhaps relief that whoever had (allegedly) done it was no longer walking the streets, and could not harm another. And I didn't have to worry about this person finding me and hunting me down, as he was now behind bars. (Because homicide is so personal, you can't help but wonder if the person who hurt your loved one will come for you, too. It doesn't make any sense, but neither does murder.) I also knew this meant there would be a trial, which I assumed would include accountability, consequences, and justice. I wondered how there could be any true reparation of harm done.

Court

In a homicide case, the body gives voice to what the dead cannot. The story of their last living moments is told by skin, bone, and blood. This was my mother's moment to take the stand.

There is nothing humane about a homicide trial. In fact, for family members, a homicide trial becomes another point of trauma. Your loved one is objectified in the impartial setting of court, as the story of what happened is told devoid of the very personal reality of what it means to you.

Justice and *the criminal court system* barely exist within the same sentence. For me, justice would be the return of my mother's life. For me, justice would be this bad guy apologizing and taking responsibility for what he did. Here is a guy who had been in and out of institutions his whole life—institutions that had obviously failed him and our society. From what I read in the newspaper, he was in foster care as a boy, juvenile detention centres as a teenager, then in and out of prison as soon as he was old enough to be tried. Why didn't anyone intervene when he was a child, when there was the possibility of him becoming something else? Doesn't anyone notice our system isn't working? It makes me angry. So tell me, how could justice within the context of these same institutions offer restitution?

It was hard to look at him, and it was hard not to. I so desperately wanted him to be sorry, but I saw nothing in his face. My first impression was that he was not in his body. That had been my impression when I saw his picture in the paper over fifteen months prior. Here he was seated before me, and yet he wasn't really there—this I could feel.

I wondered, if he goes away to the Edmonton Remand Centre, will he come out worse in twenty-five years? That had been the pattern with his incarcerations in the past, where no rehabilitation had occurred. It makes me ask again what *justice* is, and I feel stuck in the only experience of it that we have in our culture.

The media exposure felt ten times worse during the four-week trial. You lose your anonymity under public scrutiny. Often, when I used my bank card, or any card with my name on it, I would be asked if I was related to the *Salter woman who was murdered*. This went on for years. Sometimes they would mix up the details of her case, and I would find myself correcting them, as if *THIS* would do my mother justice. I would end up triggered, shaking, barely able to form a sentence. Articulating my deepest wound out loud to strangers, gave the grocery clerk or the librarian a piece of myself that they should not be privy to. This is what happens with murder. Grief, typically a private family affair, becomes the property of all who are touched by it. I ran out of many stores in the first few years, wiping away tears as their questions brought the trauma of homicide back to me.

***

The beginning of a trial often presents a timeline of events. At Brighteyes's trial, it sounded like this:

8:15. Three blocks away from the parkade, a co-worker walking to work waved to Mom, and Mom honked back.

8:15-8:20. A man went in the front door of the building and thought he heard a woman's voice shouting or screaming, "Leave me alone, just leave me alone." He could not tell where it was coming from.

8:15-8:20. Another man walked through the front door and to the bottom of the stairwell to await the opening of the barbershop. The zipper on his parka was jammed, so he attempted to remove the parka over his head. As he had it up over his head, he thought he heard a woman scream for help. He pulled it back on to hear more clearly and heard another scream for help. He thought the sound was coming from upstairs, so he started to ascend the steps to investigate. He heard one more scream, and then it stopped. He was unable to determine where it was coming from.

8:40. Two of Mom's co-workers see gloves and her briefcase on the ground in the parkade. Her truck is not there.

9:00. Her briefcase is brought upstairs and identified by co-workers.

Once the timeline was established, all of the cops or civilians who had anything to do with any of the scenes involved testified regarding the parkade, the truck, and the farmhouse. The cops especially were questioned to ensure no evidence was contaminated. Their testimony included detailing the clothing seized from Brighteyes when he turned himself in.

It was also noted that there was more than one fingerprint belonging to Brighteyes at the scene.

Around the fourth day of the trial, the medical examiner testified and shared his report. I didn't go to court on this day, as it was just too much for me take in.

Details from his report were as follows:

- Cuts to hands and arms indicated she was fighting off a knife-wielding attacker.
- Massive blood loss from a bone-deep slash in the neck severed the artery that carries blood to the brain and voice box. The slash was described as a gaping centimeter-wide horizontal cut that nicked a neck bone.
- A second large cut beneath the first severed her esophagus.
- Another neck bone was broken by a separate act.
- A long skull fracture at the back of her head contributed to her death, but it would not likely have killed her on its own. This fracture and the accompanying facial bruises were likely caused by a single act of considerable force. This blow would likely have left her unconscious, and the blood loss would probably have caused her death in about 10 minutes.
- Evidence of post-mortem rodent activity. (In other words, as she was lying in the farmhouse for ten days, mice chewed on her.)

- She was wearing her blouse, which was ripped open in front, and her bra, which was cut open in front. Both were heavily bloodstained.
- Other bloodstained clothing items were found at the scene and identified as hers.

Over the next few days, a blood-splatter expert testified, describing my mother's last 20 minutes of life, including how she fought and where she stood outside her car, what took place during the fight, where she had been in the truck, how she bled out, and where she was likely raped. Remember, this is pre-CSI; there was nothing on television in the late 1990s that gave the average person any idea of this type of evidence analysis. Based on where and how the blood landed, he detailed her struggle for life. In his testimony, she was referred to as "the blood source." When he described her being moved from one part of the truck to another, he said "the blood source was tipped and loaded," and her death was described as "termination of an active blood source." We learned that she was most likely raped after she was dead.

How do we even begin to unpack details like this and return to normal life? How do we take this information in and integrate it without breaking apart permanently? My only answer for these questions now is the evidence that somehow I did. I think our bodies take in what we can process at the time, and the rest arises as we work through the layers of our grief and trauma. I did not read the medical examiner's report or go through the notes of the trial until 20 years had passed. Instead, I sat with what I did recall, inclusive of all the newspaper articles and family conversations, and then, when I was ready, piece by piece I faced the rest.

There was an important moment of humanity in the trial when a girlfriend of Brighteyes testified. She had been with him the night before, and courageously shared how much alcohol he had consumed, as well as his lack of sexual satisfaction from their partnering, despite many attempts. He was angry when he left her apartment, which was two blocks from the parkade. The knives that were used to kill my mother came from her kitchen.

In Canada, there must be sexual assault, confinement, or kidnapping for a first-degree murder conviction, and we had all three. This meant he would have no chance of parole for fifteen years, and would likely be confined to twenty-five years in prison.

Trauma as Medicine

After the testimony came a challenge. The defence challenged the Canadian Charter of Rights and Freedoms, stating that the collection of DNA evidence from Brighteyes while he was under warrant (a gentle cheek swab; the video was shown in court) was a violation of his rights. Specifically, they charged that it "violates Brighteyes' right to a fair trial by using his own bodily fluid to convict him. It's also an unlawful seizure, because it violates his bodily integrity and affronts his dignity by going beneath the skin." This meant that the trial was put on hold for two weeks while there was a trial within a trial to address this challenge.

After listening to what happened to my mother and comparing it to the image of this perpetrator getting a cheek swab and hearing it described it as *an indignity that violates his bodily integrity,* I was speechless. Or screaming. Or both. I did both, but the screaming took some years to arrive.

Finally, after the two-week charter challenge, on April first the judge ruled that the 1995 DNA-collecting law—which allows police to get a warrant from a judge entitling them to use any force necessary to take DNA from a suspect—is constitutional. He found that the law does violate a suspect's constitutional right not to incriminate himself, but he concluded that the violation is justifiable. He said, "The limitations are reasonable and can be justified, and are not inconsistent with the constitution of Canada."

On April 8, 1997, Peter John Brighteyes was found guilty without a doubt of first-degree murder. He was sentenced to twenty-five years in jail with no chance of parole for fifteen years.

To my surprise, the verdict did not give me the sense of closure I thought it would. It didn't take away the pain or change the circumstances. There was no sense of restoration or feeling of justice. It did mean an end to the media sensationalism, but the grief was just as desperate and painful the day after court as it was the day before.

Brighteyes was taken to the Edmonton Remand Centre. Seventeen days later, on April 25th, 1997, he hung himself with his shoelaces by attaching them to a coat hook. Apparently the coat hook was designed to collapse under pressure, but he had rigged it to hold his weight. This felt so pointless to me. I did not understand the meaning of it at all. Two people dead for no apparent reason.

I could, however, accept that I was fully immersed in the underworld. I didn't have to hold it together, so willingly and intentionally, I allowed myself to fall apart.

* * *

Journal excerpt post trial.

Justice a Frank Stranger

Stricken from the record
My heart

Lost in a foreign address
An idea landing location

Tied to a landscape unfounded and unfathomable

Something that is no-thing that is not

Justice, like murderers' breath on a frozen wind in summer
Justice, like ravens' song as they fly to bring the tides of winter
Justice, like blood on bone mistaken for hunger

What is justice I wonder
As I fall from wings of explanations no longer buoyant

Forcing meaning onto meaninglessness
Choice to the choiceless

Drowned by the fanaticism of self-assurance I breathe blue

I am no-thing
I have no-thing

I flounder from heights of understanding to chaos where acceptance is the only vessel that floats

My mind an angry reel of questioning

What if we are actually wandering around in the dark blindly?
And luck is the lackluster of light
Fast food for the foolhardy

Justice a frank stranger
A dark ranger
Empty manger
Playing with danger

What if you were simply helpless
There is no purpose to it
And you died

What if this is the truth?

Murder the witness to your last minute's desperation
Reaper of your liberation

That moment your spirit was set free on the other side of rape and violence. Your body a torn map marking your exit

I wonder what I am reconciling? Who am I saving?

Myself, you, your killer?

Lost in the rhythm of sound— —tuneless

I taste the sour spill of rotten fruit

And swallow whole

***

Before you is the invitation to stop, pause, take a deep inhale, and exhale.
Again.
And again.

    Letting that sweet medicine of air move into each of your cells and touch the parts of you that may be breathless from listening to this tale and whatever it has awoken within you. Even for myself, as I read it and share it for the umpteenth time, I, too, must stop. Remind myself to get grounded as I go through the sharing, the reading, knowing the mark trauma leaves in its wake.

We all have a story of trauma, whether it is a specific event, like the one I have shared, or a compilation of many. Whether you deem it as significant as murder or whether you have tried to pass it off as irrelevant, it is not. If it calls out to you in your silent moments, it matters.

At some point on our journey of awakening, we come to realize that healing ourselves is more important than our fear of what happened or our fear of what will happen if we *go there*. In this moment, the route to address it is determined. These moments are portals of possibility, rich with the resources required to venture into our own underworld.

You will know, in that knowing part of yourself, when the time is right. This is a primordial call to own your power. To claim your whole self, you must unravel the complex story of who you are and strip away false pretenses, masks, and illusions by willingly entering the realm of your greatest pain.

PART II:

The Journey

CHAPTER 3:
Approaching the Underworld

> "The message from the Beings of the Stars is that it is necessary for everyone to open their hearts to the truth of the Spirit, of the Spirit World, as it is this truth that will lead us to our salvation"
>
> *–Grandmother Clara – Grandmothers Counsel the World*

> "Only when we are brave enough to explore our darkness will we discover the infinite perfection of our light."
>
> *–Brené Brown – The Gifts of Imperfection*

In the aftermath of trauma, it feels like nothing is certain, other than the fact that this trauma is never going to go away. Try as we might, it is there behind every corner and through every door. The shock of our experience disarms us, leaving us searching for the route back to normal—to no avail, as this *is* the new normal. The choice before us is: do we run, or do we lean in?

To lean in, we need tools and resources that generate stability, because trauma is anything but stable. Leaning in asks us to return to the underworld intentionally, and our beings are hardwired to avoid another experience of potential harm. Even if what happened then is not happening now, we know that addressing it will likely illicit pain.

We must ask ourselves what conditions need to be in place to approach the underworld on purpose. When the trauma happened, we had no control over any of the circumstances. Now it is different. Our power lies in discerning what we hope to achieve as a healing outcome and how we may simulate this for ourselves.

There are two ways in which I propose an intentional revisiting of our trauma in this text: in an altered state, such as a shamanic journey or ceremony, or in real-life experiences, such as journaling, responding to fear and triggers as they arise and addressing post-trauma physical issues (an example of the latter for me would be the belly pain I experienced).

I will share examples of both avenues with you throughout this book. The former brings us into non-ordinary reality, whereas the latter takes place in ordinary reality. The difference is important, as non-ordinary reality allows us to step into the mythic to face energetics in ways that real life does not. In non-ordinary reality, we are released from the confines of the physical, and we arrive at the landscape of the soul.

To begin exploring our approach to the underworld, let us look at the following principles. I see them as the tenets that form the container necessary to face trauma. They include the beliefs and practices that I utilized in my healing from Mom's homicide, so you will see them throughout the chapters in this book. When you are ready to move into your own underworld, they will lay the foundation for you.

1. Setting intention
2. You are not alone
3. Higher purpose
4. Creating personal safety
5. Showing up for yourself
6. Getting into your body
7. Creating an altar
8. Utilizing altered states

1) Setting intention

This is the cardinal entry point to the underworld. In fact, I like to look at intention as not only the key that unlocks the door, but the talisman that guides our path.

Setting an intention is a beautiful thing, for it is an act of honouring who you are and what you want in a sacred way. To discover what this is for you in relation to your trauma, take some time to ask yourself a whole bunch of questions to stimulate the direction of your response.

Some examples of this would be:

What do you want? When you consider your trauma and the impact it has on your life, how do you want to change your relationship with it?

What would you like to see in the future that is different from now?

Do you believe you can heal yourself?

Are you willing to free yourself from the bondage of this trauma, even if you don't know how?

Are you willing to show up and do the work to heal yourself—for yourself—no matter what?

Can you set your intention to receive the help that you need to *go there*?

One of my all-time favourites is to imagine yourself on your death bed, looking back on your life. What story do you want to tell about how you dealt with this issue?

Intention is important. It directs the energy of your focus and calls in your helping spirits and Spirit. It is a statement of power: *I am going to heal this wound*, and when you commit to it, the universe responds with what you need to move forward on to your path. This might not always look like fun. Often the initial results are different than what we thought they would be, and we need to be open to this. Good intentions include being willing to be with what arises when you ask for help and not trying to control the outcome. We need to have faith in ourselves and hold our connection to our intention at our core, knowing that we will generate what we need to face the dark step by step, rather than giving up when it gets too intense.

When you set an intention, be clear with what you are naming, because words have power. You are the alchemist who is drawing what you wish from the ethers of possibility. Give yourself permission to go for it.

Examples of clear intentions:

- My intention is to sit with my anger towards this perpetrator who... (did what to you).
- My intention is to resolve a trauma (say what it is) from my childhood.
- My intention is to face the fear I have of (name it) because of (name the experience).
- My intention is to feel my unresolved grief.
- My intention is to make medicine from my trauma.

Sometimes I have had clients set an intention such as "My intention is to love myself," which is perfectly fine and clear on its own. What happens on occasion is that when the dark stuff comes up—all of the elements that get in the way of self-love—they back away with fear, victim-thinking, and lack of personal ownership. They think, "Hey, I want to love myself, not face all of this crap." Make a note to yourself that this path is not going to be fluffy and filled with rainbows and magic unicorns cantering around you. (Not to say this can't happen...) When you set your intention to address your trauma, you will be looking at the most difficult aspects of your life, your personality, and the way you see the world. This is the point of transformation. I encourage you to allow yourself to go through the processes offered in this book to move into your darkness.

Exercise: Intention setting

Set an intention to use throughout this book. Don't worry if there is more than one thing you want to work on. There is always enough time for what we need to do in this life. You can reapply the concepts and the exercises in a second round, or a third, or a fourth, as needed.

What you need: a stone from outdoors. Read and follow the instructions below before you go find it.

1. Name the trauma you want to heal.
2. Turn it into an intentional statement and say it out loud to yourself a few times, feeling it on your tongue and in your body until you are certain you have the correct words.

3. Go for a walk outside, asking to find a stone that will help you in healing this. (You are asking your own intuition, your guides, and Spirit to lead you in this stone hunt.) Any stone will do, what is important is that you find it in nature, intentionally without buying it. As you walk hold the energy of your intention in your body, maybe even repeating it in your mind, or out loud like a mantra. Let this energy direct you to the right stone.

4. When you connect with a stone you are attracted to, ask it if it is the right one before assuming. The stone people do like to be respected this way. Let it know your intention and that you are seeking a stone to represent this issue. Does it want to help? If you get the sense that it does, make an offering of gratitude on the ground in exchange for the stone. (Check out Appendix for information on offerings.) If not keep looking until you do.

5. Once you have your stone, say your intention again out loud three times, and after each time, blow the energy of your statement into your stone. Do this by literally bringing the stone up to your lips and pulling your breath from your belly.

Keep this stone with you at all times. Sleep with it, have it on your person, and place it on your altar when you work there. If you want, make a medicine bag for it. The stone is a physical representation of your commitment to tend to this issue. Take some time to notice the symbols or markings on it that link metaphorically to what you are addressing. Is the stone smooth or rough? What is it shaped like? What does this mean to you? How does it feel in your hand? What attracted you to it? Journal about this. Be curious.

Have this stone in your hand through every exercise in this book. Each time I have you blow something into it, you are adding to its medicine as it supports your journey. It will bear the polarity of what is present—the pain of the issue and the support you need—until in time, the two come together as one.

Journal questions: Intention setting

- What happened for you with the stone exercise?
- Describe your stone and what its symbolism represents to you.
- What is your intention for healing trauma with this book? How does it feel to have stated this out loud?
- What aspects of your trauma do you tend to avoid?
- What are you afraid of?
- What happens when you visualise yourself at peace, with the sensation that this issue is thoroughly resolved and integrated? Notice how this affects your nervous system. Take a few moments, or more if needed, to imagine this.

2) You are not alone: calling your team to the table

The unseen forces around you are conspiring to help you through this. You are, and always have been, supported. This does not need to be made conscious to manifest; in fact, you don't even have to know it is happening. However, the results are magnified a hundred times when you do. Use your personal power to invoke, pray, converse with, and be present to the energetics of the universe.

Realizing you are not alone releases the pressure and responsibility of having to do it all by yourself—and makes it way more interesting.

We are products of our beliefs and an integral co-creator of our reality. If you believe you always have a team of guides and allies supporting and communicating with you, then that is what you will experience. If you believe that is not possible, or it only happens for others, then that, too, is what you will experience. You get to pick.

Let's take time to consider who these supportive forces are, and how you can play an active role in your relationship with them.

Spirit and Mother Earth

Healing is the act of coming into union with wholeness—the whole of this universe and the omnipresence of Spirit. Trauma and grief give us the impression that we are separate from Spirit, which is magnified by our pain. This fosters a sense of division that is reconciled primarily through the choices we make along the way. In the early stages after trauma, we question, "How can there be such a thing as a holy and wise universe when this can happen to me? How can both exist within the context of the whole?" This is a common human struggle, and it might initially leave us feeling abandoned or neglected by Spirit.

What became apparent to me through time is that we cannot heal trauma without divine support. As much as we do not understand why something happened, the perspective and grace of Spirit is required for us to tackle our soul wounds. We need the omnipotent point of view of the highest consciousness of the universe to lead us. This way, the truth—*I don't know what to do, please help me with this*—may be asked, spoken, and written down. This mantra, this prayer, is needed before you can fully open to what help is present. It doesn't mean it wasn't there before; but when you ask, you demonstrate to Spirit that you are humble and ready to receive a higher level of help. Healing becomes a conscious collaboration. Spirit responds to your questioning through sensations (prompts in your gut, heightened emotional responses, or a sense of knowing) that keep you actively participating in your healing. Sometimes you will receive messages in dreams, symbols in waking life, or visions from altered states.

When we realize ourselves as part of something greater, we can surrender our ego and invite this power—which is sourced in love—to fuel our approach to healing. Waking up to the energy responsible for the holiness and sacredness of life helps us name *ourselves* as holy and sacred. We need to know that what has happened in our lives is holy and sacred—even trauma.

One of the best ways to feel the energy of Spirit is through your relationship with Mother Earth. They are interchangeable in their capacity to guide our healing. Both are necessary. I encourage you to get outside on the land and lie down upon the Mother Earth—on your belly if possible—and breathe with her. Imagine that on your inhale, you can pull the living energy of Mother Earth up through your body, and on your exhale, you send energy out from your belly into the earth. Notice the energy of Spirit rising through. Breathe for awhile and think about your intention. As you breathe, ask for help.

Journal questions: Spirit and Mother Earth

- ▶ What moments stand out in your life when you felt touched and filled by the light of Spirit?
- ▶ How does Spirit communicate with you? How can this relationship be improved?
- ▶ When you invite Spirit in to help you with your trauma, what happens?
- ▶ What beliefs guide or constrict your relationship with Spirit?
- ▶ How is Mother Earth communicating with you right now? How does she want to help you with this issue?

Helping Spirits and Guides

Our helping spirits are a team or council of allies composed of power animals, mythical beings (such as gods and goddesses, angels, plant spirits, stones/crystals, archetypes, etc.), and ancestors.

Our guides are endless resources for healing, drawing from the symbolic mythos that speaks right to the centre of our soul. Some of our helping spirits have been with us from birth; some are from lifetimes past and future. Some join us for specific situations, and others stick around for the whole ride. The methods for connecting with them are infinite, and they are influenced by traditions, culture, and personal preference. What is important is recognizing that these relationships are built over your lifetime. They are not a quick one-off, and just like any other relationship, they take time, energy, and investment to develop.

You most definitely have guides trying to get your attention. You might dream about an ancestor who has passed or keep thinking about a particular archetype; this is how they talk to you. It is common for power animals to appear repeatedly in the natural environment around you, or even on your cereal box—Spirit has a sense of humour. Look for synchronicities disguised as coincidence and get curious about what they mean to you. Sometimes you might "just know" they are there—that's how it often works for me. If it is a new guide, I take time to go on a shamanic journey or do some personal inquiry in my journal to discover what their appearance is about and if it is a relationship that warrants my attention.

Some people still have a hard time connecting—which is not unusual, as we are taught to ignore our sensory perception from the time we are small. To hone in on your relationship with Spirit, you need to trust that you have your own ways that will develop in time. For now, follow the guided exercise at the bottom of this section entitled "Connecting with a Helping Spirit" for support.

> "The healing is not accomplished by or because of you alone. When you know that you are part of something larger with other perspectives to take into account, then healing feels like a joyful dance with a diverse array of partners keeping it endlessly interesting. Whether you perceive your spirit guides or totems as inside you or separate from you, when you honour and allow their intelligence to enhance your healing work, new opportunities and possibilities present themselves. You are no longer limited by your own skill; you can take advantage of the natural abilities and talents of other life forms."
>
> –Nicki Scully, *Alchemical Healing*

Communicating with our guides requires finding a common language. Often this includes asking questions and listening intuitively for answers, which may not come in words. One of the most profound ways of learning from a power animal is to ask permission to shapeshift into its body, and then look at the world, yourself, and the issue at hand through their point of view.

Their perspective in healing trauma is insurmountable. Trauma cannot be broken down and analyzed by the rational mind—we inevitably get stuck there. We can, however, communicate with our guides to gain information or a new vantage point that helps us discern what we need to do or work through.

To maintain a reciprocal relationship with your guides, you must give back. It cannot be a one-way ride, or it will not last. Guides need gratitude. This can be in the form of leaving offerings on the land (see Appendix) or sitting with them in meditation and sharing gratitude from your heart. Ask and they will tell you! You can ask your guide for specific details on how you can give back to or feed them during a shamanic journey or in meditation.

Guides can show up unexpectedly in random situations that don't make sense to our rational mind. Remember, our job is to be receptive, listen, and allow before judging and assuming. A good illustration of this comes from my first trip to the Amazon in Peru in 2009, where I went to work with Ayahuasca. During one of my ceremonies, I had a strong visitation from Jesus. It was really powerful and important for me, until my logical mind kicked in and literally threw him out of my ceremony. (Who does that to Jesus? I mean, come on!) What was happening in my head was a narrative that said, "What are you doing here? I am in a shamanic ceremony in the Amazon to experience traditional indigenous healing, and you do not belong!" I couldn't have been further from the truth. My brain, trying to organize information under certain headings, severed me from the insight I was receiving from this holiest of guides. Receiving help from Spirit requires an open mind. The need to judge, compartmentalize, or analyze who is showing up will limit what you receive.

Bone Womyn

I began to work diligently with the archetype of the Crone within a few years of Mom's death. I was familiar with her representation through the cycle of the waning moon, where she bears the silver scythe that reaps the harvest. She is a harbinger of death, helping us face the truth of loss as an inevitable outcome. I was enchanted by the Old Woman character in Anne Cameron's *Daughters of Copper Woman*, and the Bone Woman in Clarissa Pinkola Estes' story "La Loba," from *Women Who Run with the Wolves*. These characters expanded my personal understanding of the Crone, and unveiled a guide who led me through some of the most difficult parts of my healing. She goes by Grandmother Bone Womyn, and it is through her support that many of the processes I share in this book have come forth. She is a guardian of the underworld, and it is likely that you will feel her presence through the reading of this tale.

Journal questions: Helping spirits and guides

- ▶ Who is on your team? Do you know, or have a feeling about, what helping spirits and guides are available to help you on this journey? If not, practice the visualization exercise after the Ancestors section (which is next), and determine who is present to help you with this specific issue.

- ▶ Are there certain plants, animals, stones, landscapes, archetypes, etc. that call to you these days? How is this call related to your trauma? Notice the connection. In what ways will they help you heal?

- ▶ What's your best method for communicating with your helping spirits? Do you need to learn new methods? If so, what could they be? How do you give back to and honour each one you are aware of?

Ancestors

We each have three lineages of ancestors: those of our bloodline, those of our soul path, and those of the land we live on or are in relationship to.

- **Bloodline.** These are the folks whose genes you carry, whose hopes and dreams (as well as repressed trauma and emotions) impact how you relate to the world. Oftentimes, the trauma we hold has been passed down through these generations. It is up to us to heal it inside of ourselves so the line is cleansed. Ask your relations for help with this. Even those who were lost in trauma in their human form may be an undeniable source of wisdom when they have crossed over. Take time to tune in to anyone you have been curious about or attracted to. See what stories you can acquire about them from those who are living.
- **Soul path.** These Ancestors are the ones who came to this planet with a similar purpose to yours. They are your soul family, your tribe of teachers, elders, and allies, whose sole intention is to support you in aligning with your reason for coming. Though they are usually not blood relatives, they can be. They hold many keys on your path, and building a relationship with them will deepen your sense of meaning and help you step into your power. Grandmother Bone Womyn is an example of an ancestral guide from my soul path.
- **This land.** The keepers of the land—the first stewards—are the guardians of the physical location you live on. They help you come into balance with the earth, air, water, and fire. You may ask them for help in finding a place that holds the right vibration or frequency to balance your energy field, be that in ceremony, day to day life, or in practicing the exercises in this book. Perhaps you will be drawn to sit against a tree and write in your journal, to climb a mountain and hold a ceremony, or maybe you lie beside a body of water and practice shamanic journey. Inquire, listen, and follow through with how these ancestors guide you and where they suggest you spend your time in nature. It's important to make offerings to give thanks for where you are and for the abundance that is present. Typically, these ancestors are First Nations, and a relationship with them includes educating yourself about the history of the land and those who have stewarded it for generations.

Journal questions: Ancestors

- How does this trauma interact with your bloodline's history? Does it correlate more strongly with your mother or father line, and how? Do you sense or wish for an ancestor from your bloodline to guide you? If yes how may you build this relationship?

- What ancestors from your soul path are present and how may you be more open to their support?

- Who are the First People of the land you live on? Where in nature do they guide you to go for healing? What messages do they have that relates to your trauma?

- Which Ancestor(s) are most clearly supporting you right now?

Exercise: Connecting with a helping spirit

Sit down in a comfortable position, taking some deep, cleansing breaths. Hold the intention stone from the first exercise in your right hand.

Notice the sensation in each part of your body that connects with the ground. Imagine you can send roots down into the Mother Earth. Allow yourself to feel held and supported. Take a few moments as needed to do this.

Breathe into any part of your body that holds tension. With three strong exhales, breath out a "HA" sound.

Allow your breath to return to normal.

Feel the sensation of your original intention in your stone and begin to call this sensation into your body. Take some deep inhales and exhales as you observe how your awareness of this sensation changes your inner realm.

Make a decision inside of yourself to connect with the most important helping spirit, power animal, or ancestor who is waiting to guide you with this issue. It is important that you feel the energy of asking for help within yourself.

This being will automatically connect with you, simply from your asking. You might notice this connection as a sense of knowing, a sound, a visual image, or the actual feeling of their presence. Allow at least ten minutes.

When we are new to this, it might feel like the experience is more contrived by our minds than by Spirit. Trust yourself; this is how we learn to listen. We do need to engage our imagination, and this might begin in the mind, which is okay.

Allow a few minutes to pass as you tune in and notice who is present.

This guide will give you a sense of love and strength. That is always a measure of knowing if it is the right one.

Take a moment to connect your heart centre to their heart centre.

Ask why they have come forward to help you, and what you need to know about your trauma that you have not been able to see yourself. Take time to listen and sense the answer.

Ask how you can connect with them in your day-to-day life. What must you pay attention to? Take time to listen and sense the answer.

Finally, ask how you can give back to them as a means of reciprocity. Take time to listen to the answer.

When you are complete, gather all the energy from the experience into your breath, and blow it into your stone with three strong exhales. This adds the support of your guide's energy into the stone, alongside of your original intention.

If this method does not work for you the first time, give it a few more tries. If you are still struggling after that, pull a card from a power animal deck or archetype deck, and apply the same process to it.

Find something that represents this guide—an image, an article from nature, a carving—and place it on your altar (more on alters coming in this chapter).

3) Higher purpose

The next principle I want to discuss is the awareness that there is a higher purpose for our trauma. There is a feeling we get when we sense meaning and value in our hardship. It alleviates the notion that there is waste or senselessness, even if what we are doing is attempting to find sense in the senseless. Discerning a reason for what has come to pass in our lives reminds us that we are connected to the greater picture. We are, in fact, part of the life force. Spirit is inside us, and somehow, in the grand scheme of things, there is an essential purpose for all of our suffering—even if we don't know what it is.

This sense of purpose becomes the lifeline that holds what we are discovering together as we venture into the underworld. It is a reference point, as what we discover when we feel our emotions, face our fears, and learn how to metabolize our experience often does not initially make sense. Without a connection to higher purpose, we find ourselves floundering in the dark, losing our capacity to navigate. A sense of higher purpose helps us digest what is arising without needing the rational mind's approval.

I needed Mom's death to matter as much as I needed her life to matter. Thus far in my life, I had witnessed a cosmic order in the chaos or pain of being. When I looked into the forest filled with saplings, old grandmother trees, and rotting tree trunks, there was nothing I saw that did not belong. There was a purpose for every part of the cycle. The winds that snapped trees in half and the fungus that grew through decomposing leaves and soil filled me with a profound sense that there was a place for everything. This meant there was a place for my trauma, too, as an integral component in the cycles of my life.

This is related to the idea that "Everything happens for a reason" or "There are no accidents." In fact, those were two of my mother's favourite sayings, and after she passed, I kept hearing them in my head. Honestly, her spirit was louder in death than in life, and she constantly repeated those sayings in my ear, particularly when I had moments of doubt or despair.

> Sarah...
>
> > Believing it is seeing it
> >
> > Follow your gut
> >
> > There are no accidents
> >
> > Everything happens for a reason
> >
> > We choose everything
> >
> > There are no bad people
> >
> > If I believe I'm safe, I am

Of course I argued with her. The circumstances of her death most definitely made me question my beliefs and whether *any* of them were true. I found myself perpetually disagreeing with her in my head. "For God's sake, Mom! You were *murdered*. You were not safe! Your gut told you to park your car on the street, and then it was broken into a week before you were killed, so you started parking it back in that creepy parkade, and then you were attacked trying to get out of it! How could there be a reason in this? How could there be no bad people when you were murdered by one? How could there be a choice in this?"

Still, these sayings became mantras for me, despite the conflict they evoked—or perhaps because of it. I found myself curious about them. What if they *were* true? This possibility bore greater resonance for me than the alternative: that things happen from bad luck or being in the wrong place at the wrong time. Those didn't sit well with me. Plus, in all honesty, my mother's spirit was so insistent that I tune in to what the potential higher picture was saying to me that I went for it.

Journal questions: Finding higher purpose

- What happens when you imagine that there is a purpose to your trauma?
- What beliefs do you hold about why trauma happens?
- Do those beliefs help or hinder your healing?

4) Creating personal safety

The next component in preparing for the underworld journey is feeling safe, and knowing that you can move at a pace that is right for you. If triggers or content become difficult, check in with yourself and ask what you need to feel safe. Even if you know you must examine the trigger and you want to face your fear, do it in a way that is kind and gentle. It is not necessary to be hardcore.

You need to be your own authority on how you address your trauma. This is difficult, because likely you haven't done it before. However, your instinct must take precedence over another's. There may be amazing human guides to help you on the way, such as therapists, healers, and teachers, but you must use your own sensory awareness to move into what is showing up, yourself, step by step. Nobody knows what you need more than you do.

Our culture does not value moving into grief or trauma and setting up camp. There is an expectation to get over it and resume regular functioning as soon as possible. Yet experiences are not simply hurdles to jump over. It is not a race, and there is most definitely no prize at the finish line, because there *is* no finish line. So it is important to surround yourself with people who respect the value of what you are facing. While you are opening up and exploring who you are now and what it means to you, you need people who won't judge you.

Protection

There are as many guidelines in energy healing for how to protect yourself, from whom, in what circumstances, and with what tools as there are stars in the sky. It is often believed that protection is necessary to a healthy practice. This is a subject area where I tend to differ from popular opinion.

The notion of protection insinuates that there is something you need protection from. In these particular circumstances, you are moving into your own pain and trauma. This is your stuff. There is only yourself and what you make of it to fear. To heal yourself, you must trust your capacity to be with your darkness, even if this is an experience of evil. You have already taken it in to your energy body. What you are doing now is learning to metabolize/digest its impact. That being said, if you do not feel safe, identify what you need to change so that you do.

I teach my students that the ultimate protection is your capacity to love yourself and embody the light of the divine. When you know without a doubt that you are the holiness of Spirit, you can trust your instincts, set healthy boundaries, and forge fearlessly into the depths of your soul.

Of course, there are times (likely daily) where we simply cannot hold that; such is the human experience. We have moments where there is doubt, we feel fallible, and we need an extra boost. This is why we have prayer and invocation at the onset of an intentional practice: to ask for help and call in our guides. It's also why we smudge or begin with some type of physical purification ceremony (see my description for smudge/purification below, under Altered States).

The need for protection is also related to whether you tend to take responsibility for other people's stuff, or place the need to please others over the need to please yourself. This creates poor boundaries, where you take in energy you don't need or lose energy that you do. I go into more detail about this in the energy body exercises in the following chapters, and practicing them will give you a clear sense of what is yours and what is not. That is also a type of protection.

It is important to note that when you have conversations with Spirit—getting to know your guides or communicating with the ancestors—the ones who are helpful for you will give you a sense of love and support. If you find yourself conversing with critical or negative beings, they are not your guides. Set boundaries. Nobody gets to be part of your team unless they are coming from a place of kindness. It's that simple.

The same is true when listening to your gut instinct. The voice of your instinct is not critical or judgmental—that is the voice of fear, ego, and unresolved pain. Practice the exercise in Chapter 6 on Intuition and Fear, which is about how ego gets in the way of intuition.

Journal questions: Protection

- What is required for you to feel safe moving into your trauma? Consider location, time of day, who is present, state of mind, state of body (I always do better healing work after a yoga practice, for instance) and even the framework in which you will hear yourself, such as non-judgmental, non-critical, patient, loving, and open-minded.
- Which environments (and/or people) in your life do *not* offer you safety or support for this journey?
- How do you know when you are safe? In what way does your body communicate this to you?
- What gives you the sensation of being protected?

5) Showing up for yourself

I was told once by a spiritual teacher that all you need to do in life is show up—that the rest comes together in the moment, and you don't have to know what you will do or what will happen until the moment is at hand. Just be present. I found this liberating, as it alleviated the anxiety caused from projecting worry into potential outcomes.

Showing up means being present with what is here now and trusting that Spirit will provide what you need when you need it, instead of worrying over all of the details of the unknown. This is the true navigation of the underworld in your day-to-day life. It means being willing to face your fear, move through conflict, and forge new ground. It also stipulates that life itself is the process. We might set aside time, as I suggest in this text, to practice intentional exercises; this is good and often powerful. But it can't take away from the awareness that LIFE is the grand process. What you do each day from the time you get up to the moment you fall asleep is the most powerful tending of all. It can be easy to show up consciously in a workshop or a specific meditation/healing exercise, but the secret is learning how to show up in each moment and in each relationship *now*, knowing that what you need to heal or work on is always being presented to you through the ways in which you respond to life.

Showing up for ourselves is a love story of personal commitment. It is the embodied action of your pledge, "I am going to heal this no matter what, and I trust that I can."

The more you invest yourself in the process, the more you benefit from what you discover. It is a conscious choice to follow the path of freedom wherever it takes you. Trauma binds you. Showing up in the moment gives you permission to examine how, and to change or address what is necessary. This includes making space to be gentle and loving with yourself along the way, as well as persevering when the difficult and uncomfortable stuff comes up.

Journal questions: Showing up for yourself

- ▶ What does it feel like to imagine that all you need is here in this moment?
- ▶ If that were true, what would be different in your life?
- ▶ How would it change how you address your trauma?
- ▶ What specific behaviours help you show up for yourself?
- ▶ What behaviours take you away from showing up for yourself?

6) Getting into your body

To approach the underworld, you must be in your body. Trauma is stored in the cellular memory of our body on physical and energetic levels. Thus, unaddressed trauma limits our energetic range of motion and impedes our physical health. Our systems become stressed and dysfunctional, and outside resources (such as medication) become more and more essential to maintain our daily regime.

To be in our bodies, we need to be with our pain and work through what arises.

Here's an illustration of what I mean. In the winter of 1997, I was in a horrible car accident. I was a new driver, and I tried to pass someone in a blizzard in the mountains. I spun out in front of them—at one point their headlights were coming right towards me—and then I went backwards into the ditch and flipped three times, side over side. I hit hard, travelling at one-hundred kilometres per hour. Luckily, I landed on the mountain side, not the cliff side. I was still in grief from my mother's homicide and shock from the media sensationalism, as the trial was two weeks away. The car accident barely touched my radar as an important event; it was nothing compared to the upcoming murder trial.

Shock numbs our ability to connect with and be in our bodies. Sometimes it's necessary in order for us to survive trauma, but in the long run, shock will manifest in health issues as your body tries to get your attention to release the energy.

For years, I thought I was fine. In fact, my story was that nothing harmful had happened in that accident, even though I had almost died. How amazing was that!

About ten years later, I experienced a mysterious chronic shoulder issue, and my chiropractor wondered if it was connected to a car accident—apparently, it was indicative of seat-belt injuries. As I tuned into this shoulder and my right arm, it became obvious that the physical trauma was still in my body. My massage therapist could literally feel the muscle stuck to the bone in parts of my arm as a result of contracting from impact. Dealing with it required intentional action to *get into my body* with the support of massage and yoga to release the pain and strengthen the weakness.

Around the same time I was looking at this, I started to have major anxiety about driving in snowy conditions. This was the energetics of the same issue arising. I didn't live in the mountains, but I was between fifty and one-hundred kilometres from the nearest town, so I was on the highway a lot. When it was snowing, my whole body became convinced that I would die, especially if I had to pass someone. Consciously, I knew this was not true. But because it was now safe for this old trauma to surface, I was filled with panic and anxiety. Until that moment, I had never been in a position to look at the fear or the true context of what had happened. Despite the power of this fear, I made sure I didn't shy away from winter driving. Instead, I coached myself out loud while driving ("Sarah, you are safe, you are going to be okay; you've got this...") and breathed deeply (in to the count of four and out to the count of four... again... in to the count of four and out to the count of four...) so I could be certain I was in my body, not in my head, and gain the confidence I needed to override the story. This is an example of consciously going into the underworld in the day-to-day.

What is interesting to note is that because Mom's homicide overpowered this accident, I was not able to notice how it impacted my body until I addressed the more primary trauma of her death. The deeper we go into our bodies, the more we discover layers of pain that have been stored over time and experience. Each one needs to be acknowledged in its own time.

Sometimes it's helpful to hold conversations with the parts of your body or organ systems that are not well or are holding tension. You can do this by journaling and pretending that your stomach, for example, is able to respond to your questions and tell you why it is so upset all the time. Or your shoulder can let you know what it needs to gain more mobility. Perhaps an old skin condition has energetic roots in the fear of being seen, or the need to set healthy boundaries. Our bodies are talking to us all the time. If we deflect and ignore the messages, we stay stuck in our heads. If we respond and listen, we begin to sense, feel, and heal.

It goes without saying that the benefits of receiving support from body-focused therapists, ceremonialists, and energy healers are deep. We truly cannot do this all by ourselves, despite the accolades we may give to our independence. Healing asks that we get vulnerable and make ourselves receptive to getting help. Allowing someone else to hold space for us and offer expertise is a potent part of the experience.

Any physical practice that helps you move beyond the ramblings of the mind and lands you in the presence of the body is indispensable. When you feel strong on a physical level, it clears your mind and heightens your focus. Then you are able to tune inwards to physical complaints and observe how they are connected to your trauma. This is synonymous with being grounded. Consider the opening prayer I used in this book, in which you send your roots down into Mother Earth. Just the visual sensation of sending roots down facilitates groundedness. The energy body exercises shared throughout this book are also helpful for learning to be present and direct your attention towards what your body is trying to tell you.

Some suggestions for getting into your body and out of your head are:

- Body-focused therapy
- Yoga
- Dance
- Meditation
- Journaling
- Breathwork
- Smudging
- Exercise
- Time in nature
- Ceremony

Journal questions: Getting into your body

▶ What helps you be in your body?

▶ How do you know when you are in your body?

▶ How do you know when you are not in your body?

▶ What makes you disassociate, or move out of, your body?

▶ What does your body need from you to make the practice of being in your body more comfortable?

7) Creating an altar

We are preparing for the underworld on every level. In the physical world, an altar helps you focus your intention and anchors you to your priorities. It is a significant part of integrative healing, as it holds the symbolism of what you are tending to in the realm of spirit out in the open, where you can see it each day. Its creation sets the stage for embodied healing through the experience of making it, and deepens it as you walk past it each day and consider what it means to you. You will use your altar to hold all the sacred objects that represent what you are addressing, including your stone. Place it somewhere in your house where you will see it each day and it will not be disturbed by others (aka small people).

Exercise: Building an altar

You will need objects that represent the following:

- Helping spirits, power animals, guides, ancestors (of the land you are on as well as your soul path and blood line)
- The four elements: earth, air, water, fire
- Spirit and Mother Earth
- Your intention and anything relating to your trauma
- Beauty
- Anything else that feels appropriate

You will also need a cloth that feels sacred to you, smudge (or an alternative, such as aromatherapy mist, water mist, or incense) and a table.

There are infinite objects you can use to provide the symbolism you need on your altar. These may be found in nature, such as herbs, pinecones, stones, pieces of wood, plants, or crystals. You can also use a bowl of water, candle, smudge, feathers, carved animal statues, or drawings. Sometimes I like to use cards from my tarot or other spiritual decks, or even pictures from magazines or calendars. There isn't a set of rules, aside from listening to your heart and allowing your own sense of playfulness, creativity, and connection to the sacred to come forth.

Once you have gathered everything, place your cloth on the table and arrange your objects in a way that feels right for you. Connect with your intention, and take a moment to say your own prayer for what you hope to achieve. Light your smudge or incense (or mist), and bless the objects with the smoke or spray.

Integrate your altar into your daily practice by taking time to sit with it each day. Add things as you work with shamanic journey, personal ceremony, or journal questions to address trauma in day-to-day life. This fosters a deeper understanding of what is unfolding within you. Meditate, journal, and ground yourself here.

Journal questions: Setting up an altar

- ▶ What did it feel like to create your own altar?
- ▶ What do you notice is needed for you to symbolically approach the underworld of your trauma by how you have placed the objects on your altar?

8) Utilizing altered states

There was a time in our ancestral history when our people—*all* of our people— lived in close proximity to the land, spoke their own tongue, celebrated their own customs, worshipped their own gods, and made time to venture into altered states as a means of connecting with Spirit. This was normal.

It is remembered in our blood and in our bones, even though for many of us this time may stretch far beyond what can be recollected by present generations. The truth is, every one of us had ancestors who were well aware that the spiritual realms, and the keys to enter them, were a necessary part of being alive. And each of us may call upon this collective remembering, if we choose, and discover the doorways that can be opened by altered states.

So what exactly is an altered state? It is a heightened state of awareness that connects us to Spirit. It is the result of an experience that impacts all of our senses, stimulating us to let go of our need to be in control as we surrender to embodying the energy that is present within us, often allowing collective forces to move through us. Think of ecstatic dance, drumming, chanting, ceremony, sacred plant medicine, or shamanic journeys. For a more conservative example, think of being moved into another state of mind at a live concert, or the effects of running a marathon. Each can instigate a state of being that opens you to the infinite wisdom, love, and grace that is ever-present. Each can give you the sensation that you are connected and that you belong. This is why it was utilized in our ancestry: they understood that we need a process that challenges us, marks us, and raises us beyond the limitations of the mind into the land of Spirit.

From a trauma-healing perspective, this is exactly why altered states are useful.

The altered states I want to discuss with you in most detail are shamanic journeys and ceremony. This will offer reference points for understanding some of the story I am sharing and give you the foundation for using them yourself. In Chapter 8, I will also discuss Ayahuasca.

Ceremony

Ceremony is the rich art of communing with Spirit. It is prayer in action. It is life-affirming in that it empowers us to celebrate and communicate our experience of what moves us, be this the beauty in the turning of the seasons, gratitude for the abundance that is here, or expressing our emotions—grief, pain, happiness, and joy. There are many varying contexts for what constitutes ceremony, but what we want to focus on here is ceremony that specifically helps us approach and be with our trauma. Typically, a ceremony is a structured event that generates an altered state, opens the heart to Presence, and allows for the possibility of healing. You know you need a ceremony when you want to create an experience for yourself that will help you talk to Spirit, communicate unexpressed emotions, release heavy energy, and gain a new way of seeing this issue. I will lay down the structure for a few ceremonies in this book that will entice your own creative process and support you in communicating with Spirit.

Traditional ceremonies and Medicine keepers. Before we look at the individual components of ceremony, a note about traditional indigenous ceremonies. There are beautiful ceremonies that came to us through the First Peoples of North America—the Sweat Lodge, Sun Dance, and Vision Quests, to name a few. The people who are the keepers of these ceremonies train for many years to understand the intricacies of holding the space properly, communicating with the Ancestors, and developing the skills needed to support people coming for healing. These teachings include sacred protocols, rules, and methodologies specific to a culture, and these must be honoured and respected. I share a powerful example of my experience in a traditional Chicken Dance in a forthcoming chapter. If you are called to learn about these types of ceremonies, you must find an appropriate medicine person to work with, and follow the guidelines outlined within their particular system of knowledge. It is important not to assume the rights to culturally unique ceremonies or teachings without receiving the proper training and permission.

Elements of ceremony

There are basic steps in creating your own ceremonies to generate a rooted and healthy practice. Familiarize yourself with them and explore the various creative practices you might use within each stage.

Smudging/Purification. Sacred plants are used around the world as agents to cleanse the body, mind, and spirit. They give us a sense of protection and help us get into our bodies. Examples include copal or palo santos in the Andes, frankincense or myrrh in the Catholic church, sage or sweetgrass for the First Nations in Canada, and sandalwood in India. The benefit intensifies when you have a relationship with the plant you are using, such as picking it yourself or having it gifted to you, as you pull the energy of that connection into your experience. The act of smudging also calls in the spirit of the plant you are using, so knowing its unique character and how it wants to work with you deepens the experience. It is also possible to use an aromatherapy mist, holy water, or water gathered from a sacred place as an alternative—be creative. In the Amazon, a bath with flower water is often used, and this is something that is easy to do in the privacy of your own home.

Creating sacred space: the four directions. This is prayer dressed up in the clothing of invocation. It is the act of opening to Spirit by calling in all you are in relationship with and creating a safe container for your ceremony. It includes the naming of your ceremonial intent and a supplication to the greater powers that be, so you are supported and guided in your process.

As an invitation to the presence of the divine and your helping spirits, it is best spoken aloud. In many animistic, shamanic, and spiritual practices, it includes welcoming the four cardinal directions (and sometimes cross quarters) as well as above, below, and within.

Through years of teaching, I have seen many students struggling to understand the relevance of the four directions in their personal relationship with Spirit. What is important to note is that the directions are symbolic of our connection to land and place, and we are at a time in our societies where we are inherently disconnected. To understand the directions, one must form relationship with self and the Mother Earth.

The four directions act like a navigational compass, conducting your journey through the landscape of life's core teachings: life, death and renewal. They hold mythical and mystical meaning derived from the wisdom of the land. When you call in their properties in ceremony you are inviting in what they represent based on this physical location, through your perspective, as well as that of the collective.

This interpretation is influenced by the following:
1. Macro understanding - A collective agreement – conscious or unconscious - that is depicted based on how the land informs the cultures, communities, cities, and groups who live upon it. For example: in northern Canada, the land is covered in ice and snow much of the year, in some places all year, and so we Canadians associate the north with cold, winter and darkness. This association generates the relationship of what the north direction represents; the power of stopping (cold), turning inwards (dark) and resting (winter). Because of this representation, winter also holds the power of the *in-between:* the fruits of the land have

been harvested and it is not yet time to plant the spring crops, so it is time to dream and imagine the world anew.
2. Micro understanding - A more personal association, this relationship is based on an individual's perception and experiences in connection to the land. To add to the above example, a micro component could include a landscape that is in the literal north or that you visited in the north time of the year that holds power for you. Your connection to this has value and if the relationship is strong enough you might call it in during a ceremony. On a personal level, I have a relationship with the Columbia ice fields. Though they are not quite north of me, they are cold, frozen and mighty powerful and it is in the north direction that I invoke them.

The basic structure of meaning associated with the four directions that I use in my practice - as a person living in Canada - is as follows: spring/east/birth/morning, summer/south/adulthood/midday, fall/west/death/sunset, and winter/north/in-between/midnight. When I welcome each direction in, I am calling in these attributes, and I might focus on one more than another in accordance with the intention for my ceremony. If I feel stuck in my life and need to stimulate new growth, I will emphasize the support I need from the east direction since it holds the power of renewal. If the ceremony's intent is to help a group feel safe and anchored in turning inwards and being with uncertainty, I will beseech the north direction for support, to ground us in our physical bodies, and to help each person connect with what they need to navigate and be with the chaos of the in-between.

When we consider our trauma and how we get stuck in it, the seasonal cycles are helpful metaphors for our healing. For those of us in the northern hemisphere, the west/fall of the year stands for death, and if we are experiencing grief that paralyses us, we may look to the seasons as a resource to understand what is needed from us, to be with or move this energy. First comes the letting go and facing death, then the in-between/north/winter, where we agonize over the pain and discomfort of our loss until we begin to accept it, then, in time we generate new life in the spring. This seasonal metaphor might not happen over the course of the literal seasons; there might be a few years of facing death and a few years of the in-between. What helps is knowing that the cycles are impermanent, and birth always follows.

Journal questions: Four directions

- What are the macro associations with the North, East, South and West where you live?

- Consider the following associations:
  Spring/east/birth/morning
  Summer/south/adulthood/midday
  Fall/west/death/sunset
  Winter/north/in-between/midnight
  Take time to explore your environment throughout the changing seasons to find four places that represent this energy for you. This can be as extreme as wandering out into the wilds and as simple as setting up altars in your yard; you get to choose. In each season ask each direction, "What do I need to learn from you? How can I come into a healthy relationship with your medicine? How can I give back to you?"

- What additional directional teachings are you connected to that feel important on your healing journey?

For examples of the invocation of sacred space, see Appendix. I have included detailed lengthy ones for the poets at heart as well as simple non-dogmatic prayer to appeal to those of all faiths.

Stating your intention. Why are you having this ceremony to begin with; what is the purpose? The intention for a specific ceremony is going to be little more finite than the one I have asked you to set as an overall intention in this book. It will be a micro component to the macro picture of facing your trauma. It is important that this intention is based on what you yourself can be responsible for. For example, don't set an intention that is dependent on another human being, such as "My intention is to make so-and-so see what he did wrong." This is not your work to do. You can, however, state, "My intention is to express my unresolved emotions and pain that are the result of what so and so did to me."

See the difference there? Your healing cannot be tied into what another does or does not do. This will only further entrap and bind you.

Methods and mediums. This is the central part of your ceremony. It is where you find a conduit to express the energy inside of you to the state where it culminates, maybe even into chaos, and shifts into something new. For me, this means letting myself go crazy through dance or drumming, singing, screaming, or journeying. If I am leading a group, I might add group chanting and a sacred fire circle to the drumming and dancing. Some of the most universal components of ceremony are sound tools (rattles, drum, flute, crystal bowls, etc.), singing, dancing, journeying, and plant medicine. Play with what you are attracted to and get curious about which are most suited for helping you get out of your head.

Time and space to listen. This one cannot be understated. It is the time when the energy from the above process is expressed, any struggle in the mind is released, and one can tune in more fully to the great Silence of Spirit. It often continues long after ceremony. I encourage you to allow yourself to rest in this space for as long as possible.

Closing the sacred space. Give thanks for what you've experienced by acknowledging the help you've received from what you invoked at the beginning of your ceremony and what showed up during the process.

Shamanic journeys

A journey is like a guided meditation that generates an altered state. Its intent is to connect you with the symbolic language of your soul.

What makes it different than meditation is the use of the drum, rattle, or other sound instruments to induce a hypnotic, trance-like state. This is essential in moving through the barriers of the mind into the realm of Spirit.

Non-ordinary reality is a term given to the multifaceted dimensions we visit on a shamanic journey. It is divided into three worlds: lower (which is this underworld I keep talking about), middle, and upper, in addition to your place of power. Being able to map or navigate your journey in non-ordinary reality is helpful in bringing clarity and intention to your experience of shamanic journeying. If you are new to journeying and this language feels foreign to you, receiving the guidance of an experienced shamanic or animistic practitioner will aid you in this process. Alternatively, check out the list of resources and next steps, found in the back of the book.

Place of power. This is the first place you enter via visualization at the onset of your journey, and is generally outside in nature. It may be a place you have been before, or it may be one that you are creating in the moment. It is essential that you feel safe in this space and engage all of your senses to become aware of your surroundings. Get curious here. What colour is the sky? Is it day, or night, or both simultaneously? Is there water, mountains, meadows, prairie, forest? Are there four-legged animals, or winged ones? What does the air smell like? What does the ground feel like under your feet, and what is it made of—stone, sand, soil, grass? Notice why you have chosen this space... or has it chosen you?

Lower world/Underworld. Bearing many names throughout the ages, the underworld holds the secrets to our soul's greatest hungers, for within its depths live the aspects of ourselves that have been denied, rejected, and lost, be it by ourselves or others. It is the home of our grief and our trauma.

It also holds:

- Our need to love and be loved, inclusive of all the conditioning and stories we hold around that connection
- Unresolved experiences of fear, trauma, and powerlessness, as well as their gifts and teachings
- Issues in relationships, marriage, and family of origin
- Reoccurring patterns, false beliefs, and binding ideology: the truth behind the lies we have told ourselves
- Healing for our past
- Lost parts of our soul

Nine times out of ten, we journey to the lower world. The entrance to the lower world generally appears as a hole in the ground, a cave or cavern, a door at the base of a tree, or an entrance behind a waterfall.

Middle world. We venture into the middle world when we seek answers that exist in this time and space, such as a physical object that has been lost or a greater understanding around current environmental/societal/political issues. When I am travelling for work, I often journey through the middle world to my intended destination to ask the permission of the Ancestors of that land to go there, and look for any information that might help me prepare for my program. You enter the middle world from your place of power by flying or moving over the earth.

Upper world. The realm of our highest guidance, it is here that the star nations make their council, the angels await you, and the Akashic records may be accessed. We come to the upper world when we seek the highest resolution of consciousness. Here, we may experience the teachings of great masters, goddesses, and gods of this world. We come to the upper world when we are in search of a guide. It is also used for accessing information about the future. Entry is often found through a ribbon of light leading up, a flight into a cloud-like realm, or magic carpet.

The upper world offers us external guidance, whereas the lower world offers us internal guidance. Both are relevant. You can tell when you have moved between the worlds through a sense of transition in your body.

It is important to remember that there are no right or wrong experiences. This is *your* relationship with Spirit. You are connected—we all are—so this is about learning how Spirit speaks to you, and trusting what you notice. This may be visual, auditory, a felt sense, or a sense of knowing. You are here to open the door to your spiritual self, a part of us that is often shut down in this life. Turning that part back on sometimes takes time.

One of my clients, Jane, offered the following share from her experience with shamanic journeying to address childhood sexual abuse. It is helpful to understand that journeying works differently for each of us, and that it is through tuning inwards and listening that our personal truths unfold.

Jane's Story

I spent many years feeling disconnected and disassociated from myself and the world around me. Through shamanic journeys, I have been able to find a way to heal, to forgive myself and my perpetrators.

At first, I found it hard to engage in the process of meditation and journeying. I was holding back because I did not yet trust (no matter how much I thought I could) and could not let go of my need for control. I began to realize that the vulnerable child inside of me was scared to let others see the real me.

Once I realized what was happening, I made sure to be present while I was on this journey and began to open up. I vowed to honour my inner child and my soul.

When asked to journey to meet my power animal, I was afraid I wouldn't experience anything, but I did. I feel a deep connection with my power animal. I have now invested in a relationship with him. I feel in tune with Mother Earth when I am with him. He is wise and sensitive and does not question his belonging... he just is. He talks to me in my mind and I trust him and am learning to trust myself. I am becoming my own authority.

From journeying, I have learned that I need to travel to the underworld regularly. I need freedom from the stories I tell myself. I need to have regular conversations with my demons. I needed to figure out why I felt responsible for other people's feelings and responses, because as long as I did, I would be paralyzed and would never be free. I was able to face myself and begin taking back my power.

Now, I am experiencing more authentic relationships with others. I am committed to my own soul and no longer give in to feeling responsible for others. I am embracing life and all that awaits! I know I am on the right path and feel the world opening up to me.

Jane – Camrose, Alberta, 2019

Two journeys for you

For the sake of our trauma focus, I will offer two journeys here for you to practice. The first is to establish your place of power. This is fundamental in generating your sense of safety and neutralizing your nervous system. It creates the basis for all your exploration in non-ordinary reality, and as such becomes your go-to location to get grounded, stop, and tune inwards. The second journey is into the underworld, to find information that is pertinent today for understanding your trauma. With practice, you can change or add to this intention.

Though I have described the uses of the middle world and the upper world, our plan is to venture into the underworld. The tricky thing about the journey process is that nothing is absolute. Although I am telling you that the trauma energy you want to explore will be in the underworld, there will likely be facets that contradict what I am saying and will lead you elsewhere.

I suggest that you begin to practice both of these journeys regularly. Once you get comfortable and start to trust this method of self-exploration, allow yourself to be open to guidance that might take you into the upper or middle world. Journeying is like a muscle that is strengthened with practice. You will learn to trust your instincts and know where you need to go.

Take time with these journeys. Don't rush the process. You may do them by memory after you read them through, if this is easy for you, or you could record them. Alternately you can have someone read them to you out loud, or if you desire, they are available for purchase on my Website (www.sarahsalterkelly.com). If you are doing it yourself, find a journeying drum track online to play. Most people find it easier to journey with the sound of the drum and lying down. This is not true for everyone. Some people need to be standing and swaying, and others prefer to drum for their own journeys. Some use no drum at all, preferring rattles, singing bowls, or silence. Find what works for you. I will reference the use of the drum, as this is the most common practice.

With each journey, have your intention stone in your hand.

Exercise: Place of power journey

Intention: To create a safe place that will sustain and empower you in your healing journey.

> Take three long, slow, cleansing breaths.
>
> Tune in to the sound of the drumbeat, letting the rhythm work its way into each cell in your body...
>
> With each inhale, draw the energy of the creative life force right into the core of your being, and with each exhale, release any heavy energy you are holding... Do this a few times filling yourself with this vital energy.
>
> Notice the sensation of the ground beneath you at each place your body contacts it. This could be a chair, a bed, the earth, or simply the bottoms of your feet. Breathe into those places, feeling yourself held and supported...
>
> Imagine yourself lying somewhere outside in nature. This can be a place you have been before, or one you are imagining in your mind's eye for the first time...
>
> What is important about this place is that it gives you a sense of freedom, belonging, and peace. Here, you feel free to be yourself exactly as you are now, without having to suit any external ideas or ideals. There is nothing you must change or do...
>
> Notice what happens when you experience this....
>
> As you look around, get curious about your environment. Are there mountains, rivers, ocean, forest, prairie, or desert? Where are you, and what does this mean to you?
>
> Take note of the sensation of the earth beneath your feet. What is it made of? Take a moment to reach down and touch it, taste it, or smell it. (Pause)
>
> Take note of the sensation of the air on your skin... What does it feel like? Is it hot, cool, or just right? Is it humid or arid? Does it bear any scent that indicates the land it has crossed prior to becoming your breath? (Pause)

Explore the horizon of each direction, taking time to notice what is present...

Begin with the East, the place of the rising sun,

Pause, notice, and sense what is here for you...

Turn to the South, the place of high noon,

Pause, notice, and sense what is here for you...

Face the West, the place of the setting sun,

Pause, notice, and sense what is here for you.

Turn to the North, the place of midnight,

Pause, notice, and sense what is here for you...

When you are ready, find a comfortable place to sit down in this place of power...

Take three more deep cleansing breaths...

Send a root down into the earth with three more breaths...

Send branches up to the heavens with three more breaths...

Notice how you feel in this space whose sole intention is to empower you...

Gather this energy into your heart centre... you are the conduit of this power between heaven and earth...

Blow your connection to this landscape into your stone with three strong exhales.

When you are ready, return.

To integrate this experience, take time to journal what came up for you. Create a piece of art that represents this place of power. Put it on your altar.

Variations:

- Next time, call in your primary helping spirit (the one you connected with that is specifically here to help you with your trauma) shortly after

you arrive, and explore the space with them. What messages do they have for you about being rooted, safe, and grounded?
- Set up an altar in your place of power that is a sister altar to the one in your home. Decorate the area with anything your heart desires that prompts a feeling of connection, empowerment, and safety.
- Set up another altar in your place of power specifically for the ancestors. Include objects for your blood line, soul path, and those of this land. Notice what happens when you sit with this altar.

Exercise: Underworld journey

Intention: to connect with a piece of unconscious information in the underworld that will support you in addressing your trauma.

Begin by smudging yourself and connecting with your intention.

Hold your stone in your right hand.

Take three long, slow, cleansing breaths...

Tune in to the sound of the drumbeat, letting the rhythm work its way into each cell in your body...

With each inhale, draw the energy of life right into the core of your being, and with each exhale, release any heavy energy you are holding...

Notice the sensation of the ground beneath you at each place your body contacts it. This could be a chair, a bed, the earth, or simply the bottoms of your feet. Breathe into those places, feeling yourself held and supported...

Begin to breathe yourself into your place of power. Take a few moments to orient yourself here, noticing if anything has changed since you were last here...

Greet the four directions, pausing at each quarter.

East...

South...

West…

North…

Notice what is different or what has changed…

Call in your helping spirit. Connect your heart centre to theirs, theirs to yours, observing the beam of light that illuminates this connection…

They are here to help you on this journey and will support you in feeling safe and guided. Ask if they have any messages to share with you.

A path opens before you to your right, and together you move towards it.

It moves through an ancient forest of evergreen trees. As you walk, you breathe in the scent of cedar, pine, spruce, and fir. The spirits of these ancient ones are cleansing your energy body and rooting you with each step… notice how this feels….

Notice the sensation of the earth beneath your feet, the texture of the forest floor, and the sounds that surround you…

The path comes to the opening of a cave. It is like nothing you have seen in ordinary reality, for it is filled with aquamarine water, and there are symbols carved all around its entrance. You know this is a holy and sacred place. There are altars at ground level and high up on its sides, all bearing offerings of flowers, urns of seeds and grain, and effigies of power.

You know this is your entrance to the underworld.

Pausing before one of the altars, connect with your intention, saying it out loud and blowing it into your stone. (If this is your initial underworld journey, your intent is to connect with a simple piece of information that will help you in addressing your trauma today.)

Reach into your pocket and place an offering on one of the altars. Then slowly disrobe, leaving all your clothes that represent ordinary reality…

When you are ready, move into the cave with your helping spirit… Stepping into the water, gently place your palms on its surface and say a prayer to the spirits of water to carry you safely. Feel their response…

As you enter deeper, submerging yourself in the water, you are pulled by an invisible current... This river weaves its way through the dark. There are moments when you can see nothing at all. Notice how this feels as you continue to move downwards...

There is a soft light ahead, and the rushing sound of water... you are approaching some type of waterfall. There are no ledges you may climb up on, so the only choice is to move forward into the sound of water falling. You are swept with the current down a long, smooth slide of rock, landing in a vast underground cavern...

The water spreads out into a pool where you are standing. This space is lit from high above, so you can make out the stalagmites and stalactites coming from the ceiling and growing from the ground. They sparkle with crystalized minerals, adding to the ethereal glow of the space you are in.

You know without a doubt that you are in the underworld. Take a moment to get familiar with your surroundings.

Stepping out of the water, you see that there is a ceremonial outfit laid out for you on the shore. Notice its colour, fabric, and style...

Putting it on, you feel lighthearted and powerful. This clothing was made for you and it brings out a quality in you that you had forgotten. Take a moment to move around the space as you explore how it feels on your skin and what it compels you to do...

Your helping spirit guides you towards a space in the centre of this vast cavern.

There is a being standing there waiting for you... You know that this being is the keeper of the underworld. Take a moment to greet them. Engage all of your senses in this process. What does this being look like, smell like, sound like, feel like? Is there a taste in your mouth? How does your body respond to greeting the keeper of your underworld? (Pause.)

Taking a few deep breaths, reconnect with your intention for coming. Say it out loud to this guardian, asking them for help. When you do so, they place an object into the palm of your hand. This object represents the information you are seeking; it is what you came here for. Notice what it is and what it feels like in your hand. Ask the guardian for any additional information you need, such as, "What do I do with this, how do I carry this, what else do I need to know....?"

Pause, taking time to listen....

Blow all this information into your stone.

When you feel complete, give thanks to this guardian, knowing you will get to know each other well as you continue to come into the underworld for information.

Move to the water's edge and remove your ceremonial outfit. Find a place to tuck it away for safekeeping until you return....

Enter the water and swim upstream to the entrance, feeling the companionship of your helping spirit at your side....

When you reach the place where you began, pause again at the altar and give thanks. Put your ordinary clothes on. Each item makes you feel grounded and present....

Move down the path towards the common area of your place of power....

Ask your helping spirit any questions you have about your journey. Get clarification about what you were given by the guardian of the underworld as needed....

When you are ready, return.

Smudge and journal.

Variation:

- Ask the guardian of the underworld to take you deeper into its depths and show you what you are hiding from yourself or what you are afraid of.

Let's summarize what is in your stone now. It holds your initial intention, your helping spirit, the place of power, and the object from the guardian of the underworld.

Intentionally being with your trauma

Imagine the steps in this chapter like a checklist, as if your bags are packed and you are embarking on a literal journey to an unknown destination. Though the territory may initially feel foreign, you will get more comfortable after you arrive and begin to map out the landscape. Reference this chapter as you apply these concepts to what is being shared.

Ask yourself as often as needed:

- Do I feel connected to Spirit and my guides?
- Can I locate a sensation of purpose within me? If not, can I imagine there is one for the time being?
- Am I safe, in the right environment, and with the right person or group?
- Am I present in my actions (showing up) and present in my body?
- Have I created a safe space to anchor my work, such as an altar?
- Have I safeguarded time for ceremony that will not be interrupted or rushed?

Set your own pace as to how and what you address as you cultivate this intentional, conscious relationship with your trauma. Foremost is the acknowledgment of what happened and your intention to be with it. I had two statements of intent. They changed a little through the years, but basically they were, "My mother was murdered, and I will do whatever it takes to heal this" and "My intention is for freedom."

I suggest having a daily journal practice where you feel, notice, or bring awareness towards what is here now. I also suggest you utilize the exercises and techniques offered in this book in the order in which they are presented to root you in this practice.

CHAPTER 4:
Tending to the Victim

"With everything that has happened to you, you can either treat it as an obstacle or a gift. Everything is either an opportunity to grow or an obstacle to keep you from growing. You get to choose."

–Wayne Dyer

Trauma shows us our deepest vulnerability: the unpredictable nature of reality and the fact that we are not always in control. People can and will hurt us. Random events will cut us open, and at some point or another, we will lose everything we have and everyone we know, either by their death or ours. This is quite unsettling. And it is true.

When we live our lives in resistance, refusing to acknowledge the truth of our vulnerability, we expend most of our energy generating internal conflict. If instead we decide to get real, humble, and honest about our pain, we become empowered. We have no control over what happened to us, but we do have control over what we do with it.

When we take charge of how we respond to trauma, we become the leaders we are waiting for. Rather than blaming ourselves or others and waiting to be rescued, we assume the necessary authority. In this chapter, I want to explore what is needed to tend to the victim in an empowering and sustainable way, to shift away from identifying as victim and set the stage for being with what is present.

Acknowledging the victim self

This memory from my childhood is a great illustration of a victim response in the face of an unexpected, painful event. Though in many ways it was minor, it's an example of acknowledging what our victim self needs.

It was a summer day like any other, and I was out riding my bike alone in the neighbourhood. I was probably six years old, as that was around the time I got my blue bike with the long banana seat and ribbons on the handlebars. Riding alone wasn't an anomaly; I liked to be by myself and pursue adventure, and back in the early 1980s, it was normal for kids to go outside and play by themselves. (Imagine that!) What was unique about this day was my wipeout. I fell and scraped my leg on the bike pedals and on the road, and it really hurt. I recall consciously deciding to lie there on the hot pavement, in the middle of the road, until someone came to help me. I was in pain, and thought for sure that there was someone out there who would notice and do something about it. (Note that my pain needed to be seen and acknowledged.) As luck would have it, a neighbour drove up, saw me before driving over me, and stopped to see if I was okay. I remember sitting up and telling her the story of what had happened, showing her where I had hurt myself. She acknowledged my pain: "Aww, I'm sorry, let's get that cleaned up and you will be like new in no time." She took me into her house to wash my leg and get a Band-Aid™. I was way more validated than I would have been at home, as this neighbour had no kids. At home, my four-year-old brother and eight-year-old sister limited the attention administered for scrapes on the leg. I was surprised and grateful that someone cared enough to tend to my wound, even though she didn't really know me. The wounded victim inside me was thoroughly appeased, and instead of going home with the story of "Look what happened to me," expending all of my energy to get people to notice or care, instead I told a story of kindness bestowed.

In the aftermath of trauma, we can't simply lie paralyzed in the middle of the road and wait for someone else to make it better, even if we feel like it. There isn't another—aside from ourselves—who has the same interest in whether we heal. In other words, nobody cares about your outcomes as much as you do; they are too busy tending to their own issues. *You* need to care, and your pain needs to be seen, acknowledged, and validated by you and you alone.

This becomes a courageous act of reclaiming your power, because you are no longer waiting around for someone to fix your stuff; you become the one giving the needed recognition *and* the one receiving its energy.

Why it is important to acknowledge the victim self

When we ignore our victim self, we begin a pattern that blames others or external circumstances, not just in relation to our trauma, but in relation to all the circumstances that instigate a similar sensation of powerlessness. This victim self— typically a little girl or little boy within us—is activated by experiences of powerlessness and vulnerability, and often responds with anxiety, panic attacks, rage, or simply shutting everything else out. After all, she is doing everything she can to get your attention and be noticed, and her heightened response is the culmination of many experiences of not being seen. Likely there is an inner narrative of "Nobody cares, nobody ever helps me, this is all too much, I always have to do it alone, nothing ever works out for me." These reactions are based on real-life experiences from childhood where she/he/they needed tending and did not get it. To change the story within yourself, you need to change the pattern. The best way to do this is to begin with your trauma.

What the victim self needs from you

Your victim self is asking for your compassion. (I am going to reference the victim self as she or her from here on, please substitute, he, him, them or they as needed.) She is the most broken, wounded, and fragmented part of you. It is helpful to connect with her in your imagination. You can do this *at any time* by visualizing yourself drawing her forth from the recesses of your being and gathering her into your arms. She might appear as a child, or as the age you were at the point of trauma. She needs you to mother her like no one has ever done before, exactly how you imagine the Great Mother would do. Here is where you stop waiting for all of those people who should have shown up for you and didn't, and take the initiative to care for her yourself. She needs you to tell her it will be okay and that she will be taken care of. She wants you to say, "I am so sorry for what happened. I am so sorry for your pain. You were powerless. It was unfair. There was nothing you could have done to prevent it. I am so sorry. I am so sorry." She needs you to take her side.

Now, she will not always believe you, particularly if this is the first time you are listening to her with sincerity. You may need to bargain with her. What must you do to prove that you will take care of her? If you have abandoned her in the past, what will be different now? This is a personal commitment that states, "I've got you no matter what, and I will not let you down."

Giving her the attention she is due, free of criticism and judgment, shifts the dynamic of her energy in your life. She is no longer hijacking your day to point out all the things that have happened to her, because she is being seen and tended. You are no longer subservient to helplessness.

You are not what has happened to you

Tending to the victim's needs does not mean you are a victim. There is a vast difference between being victimized and living life as a victim. Once we validate that inner victim, our unconscious energy is no longer spent seeking evidence to validate our pain. You already know your pain, feel your feelings, and attend to what shows up for you.

For years, I greatly resisted acknowledging my inner victim. I so desperately did not want to be the girl whose mother was murdered… but I was. It did happen. My punk rock uber-independent nature fought this truth to the bone. I didn't want to define myself by my loss, but I was also very possessive of it, and cautious of any outsider who might try and take my grief away from me. "I mean really, don't they know what happened to me?!"

In the late 1990s, I came across a teaching that helped with this. It was in a book called *You Are That*, by the American spiritual teacher Gangaji, and the focus was on discovering our identity as that which never changes, beyond what has happened to us, the roles we play, or the identities we claim. It taught me to recognize the fallibility of "needing to be something in order to be someone." It helped me move away from the need to BE my grief and step out of the victim story. Yes, Mom's death is part of my life and impacts who I am, but it isn't *who* I am.

Expressing your victim self

Trauma changes our identity forever. We must face and let go of what will never be. Sometimes we feel like jumping up and down and screaming, "It's not fair!"—and there are moments when that is part of the process. When we're ready, each aspect of what will no longer be needs to be named, validated, and released. This is our grief work: to mourn what was so we can move into what is. This is also our victim work, as it is acknowledging and honouring the truth of our powerlessness. For me, this was letting go of the girl whose mother was still alive, because she, too, had died. When disappointment, pain, or intense grief arose, I had to feel it. Often this included exercises, practices, or ceremonies to help it along the way.

My favourite practice was to write Mom letters directly in a journal I created just to talk with her. The following excerpt was written about six years after she passed. My husband and I had recently bought our first house, and our twin girls were nine months old. Being a new mom in my new home with my new family brought so much grief to the surface.

> March 2001
>
> Dear Mom,
>
> It is one month since we moved into our first house, and I am overcome with grief for you.
>
> Today is a really hard day. I look around and see all of the things you will never see or know about me, from my kitchen table that I am writing on, to my fenced yard, the toys strewn on the floor, the clothes I am wearing... essentially who I am becoming as a mother and a woman. As I fed the girls porridge in their highchairs this morning, I marvelled over how precious they are, and then I got lost in the fact that I don't have you here to share it with. I don't know if I am a good mother. I have no idea if I am doing any of this right. I am just making it up in the moment, day-by-day, and hoping for the best. I hear you tell me to "trust my gut." I see you looking back at me through their eyes, your smile in their smiles... but sometimes, like today anyway, that doesn't feel like enough. It's not fair.

I hear my friends complain about the omnipresent focus of their mothers, of their overbearing natures or inappropriate involvement with their children, and I just want to slap them. I want to scream and shout out how lucky they are! To tell them to stop taking what they have for granted. I have no one who cares like that for my kids, aside from their father.

My soul is hungry for your stories. The stories passed only from mothers to daughters. I want to know what I ate at nine months of age. How were my sleeping patterns, and when did I stop sucking my thumb? What were my first words and favourite toys? What did you do when I was sick? How did you cope, day after day, with all of us little ones, when Dad was so often out of town? Did you go crazy? Have days when you contemplated madness over mothering? For me that is daily… and then I breathe and find a way through it. Mark is usually home by 6 p.m. and I have the reprieve you never had.

Sometimes I fantasize that there is a book somewhere that you wrote for me to answer all my incessant questions and wonderings. "This is how you potty train… When they are walking, you need to be aware of this, this, and that… Best teething remedies are… For colic, try this recipe… For a high temperature, do this… To keep yourself from going crazy you need to…"

Alas, there is no such book.

I feel like your loss makes me want to be an even better mother. Especially as a mother to daughters who bear your legacy. I want them to grow up to be strong women who will not get lost in the restricting ideas or ideals of what a woman should or shouldn't be. And even though their grandmother was murdered, I do not want them to live ruled by fear.

What I long for is that sense of knowing you were always there, even if I didn't want you to be, even if I didn't agree with what you thought or your point of view. You were still always there.

Love you and miss you Mom,

Sarah

Though this pain lessens over time, it doesn't ever go away entirely. Twenty-four years later, I can be at a café writing in my journal and notice a mother and daughter at a table nearby, and I'll still start to feel sad. My reaction is, "Aww... how beautiful. I wonder what that would have been like. How sad that it will never happen for me. I wonder what Mom would have said or done in this situation?" I allow myself to feel all of the feelings related to what is before me. This is how we tend to the victim self. There were times in the early years where my response would have been different. I would have felt like it was not fair that I would never have that. This truth might have made me angry or resentful—which was also appropriate for where I was in my grief process. I had to feel what would never be in order to let it go.

Journal questions: Addressing your victim self

- ▶ Sit in a quiet place, close your eyes, and locate your victim self inside of your body. Make a connection with her. Use all your senses: notice what she looks like, what she is wearing, etc. Is there a particular part of your body she is hanging out in? Why there?

- ▶ What does she need from you? What does she want you to see? What have you not been hearing? What is she trying to tell you?

- ▶ Write down the story of what happened from her point of view.

- ▶ What must be validated and acknowledged in order to release the hold her energy has on you?

Acceptance and the victim

Accepting the reality of what has happened is another prerequisite to assuming your personal authority. My favourite prayer of acceptance is the infamous Serenity Prayer, attributed to theologian Reinhold Niebuhr.

> God grant me the courage to accept the things I cannot change,
>
> The courage to change the things I can,
>
> And the wisdom to know the difference.

In time, our tending of the victim leads us to choose what we are willing to accept. When the expression of the wound is heard, felt, and addressed, the energy changes within you. This is because your relationship with yourself and what happened changes.

Before we can accept the things we cannot change, we go through a natural process of blame.

This includes the assumption that it was somehow our fault. You perseverate over what you should have done differently and are sure that somehow, there was something you could have done to prevent the trauma. Even when it is ridiculous to think this, we do. I know I did. I thought Mom and I were so spiritually connected that I should have known, should have seen something or had some sort of intuition that would have saved her. I felt like I failed. This was one of the victim voices I needed to tend to.

We also blame others. For me, this was initially everyone *except* her killer, as I was not ready to face him for a decade. But I did blame the owner of the parkade who didn't put in proper lighting, the people who heard her scream and didn't look for her, and the elder who said Brighteyes was fit to return to society and released him one week before he murdered her. Of course, there was also the guy who bought Mom's ring at the bar, which was obviously stolen; I blamed him, too. "How could they do that?" "What kind of a person would do that?" I was astounded by what I saw as their ignorance, complacency, or lack of responsibility.

After the blaming, reclaiming

Both aspects are important—the self-blame and the blaming of others. Both must be experienced in your personal act of truth-telling, letting your victim self use her voice. Then there comes a time where you are done with this. I find it arises organically for most people. I just got tired of hearing my own projections, and I knew they were not true.

Naturally, you start to move towards the truth: that you could not change the circumstances. Period. Nor could the other people who were indirectly involved. Somehow, this happened for a reason, even if you do not understand it, and your power lies in what you do with it *now*.

This leads us to examine the person who caused the harm (if there is a particular person in your circumstance). They could have done something differently, and they did not. How do we accept this? I unpack my experience of facing my mom's perpetrator in detail in Chapter 7. For now, I am going to offer you a pretty clichéd response, one that helped me with acceptance from the time I was a girl, because of course it was my mother who first introduced it to me. It is a quote that has been made famous recently by Brené Brown, but I am pretty sure it started with Louise Hay in the mid-80s.

> "What if everyone is doing the best they can with what they know right now?"

You might be wondering how, in the name of all the gods above, I can relate that quote to a murderer. Read on and you will see in time. For now, I encourage you to imagine that it is possible and notice how you feel when you do.

For myself, any time I am up against a moment where I feel like blaming another, or I am blaming myself, I think of this quote and I ask myself, "What if this is true? What if everyone, even me, is doing the best they can?" And typically, because when I feel powerless I feel out of control, I then ask myself what is in my power to control in this moment. *God, grant me the courage to change the things I can…*

Acceptance comes in increments. It comes by recognizing what things we think are impossible to accept and starting there. It is helpful to ask, "What do

I need to accept about this today, or what can I accept about this today?" Give yourself permission to be with what is true for you, rather than forcing it.

Journal questions: Reclaiming your power

- ▶ What have you deemed unacceptable in regards to your trauma?
- ▶ What is in your power to accept now?
- ▶ What do you need help with?
- ▶ Who is here to help you: power animals, ancestors, Spirit?
- ▶ What comes up for you when you consider the quote, "Everyone is doing the best they can with what they know right now"? Be honest.

Making boundaries

Knowing what is ours to be responsible for and what is not is an essential life skill. Unfortunately, because we live within the framework of cultures, communities, and families that do not make this a clear practice, it becomes something we must pursue and decipher on our own. We must learn to trust our own perceptions of our trauma or grief over that of another's. This requires the ability to set healthy boundaries. It is so easy to allow the opinions or ideas of others to wrongfully influence and change your point of view. When you choose their perspective over yours, you betray yourself and end up right back in the position of victimization.

A great example of this for me would be from around five or six years after Mom died, when I found myself struggling to see and feel what she would be like in my life given all that had changed since she passed. I was in my mid-20s, a young mom, a bona fide adult with a much different reality than the one I had when Mom died. I asked family members who were older than me for their opinions. "What do you think Mom would be like now?" and perhaps more importantly, "What would she think of me and my life as it has turned out?" This meant that I began to acquire perspectives based on other people's relationships with her, some of which totally contradicted the one I had had. It became paramount to remember that my connection to her began inside of *me*, not outside, from the perspective of another. Though some of their sense of her was the same as mine, there was much that was not. I had to learn how to set boundaries and say to myself, "Wait a minute; I know who my Mom is to **me,** and I can find her within me by stopping, listening, and asking her myself!"

Energetic boundaries

Having a sense of who we are—separate from the outside world—allows us to move through our lives as sovereign beings. This does not negate our connection to the ALL of the universe; in fact, the opposite is true. It allows us to focus inwards first. Within ourselves, we find the ALL.

This means forming a relationship with your energy body. It is a foundational tool for setting healthy boundaries and harnessing your power. As you develop this relationship, you become discerning about what external energy you choose to take in, and you become aware of the futile ways in which you expend, leak, or give energy away. If you find yourself spending too much time and effort trying to say the right thing, please others, or honour another's perspective on what happened over yours, you have weak boundaries, and this practice is of the utmost importance for you.

Our *energy body* is synonymous with the terms *light body* or *energy bubble*. It is influenced by your connection to the natural world around you and is sourced in your capacity to embody love. As your unique expression of the creative life force, its vitality depends on your relationship with self and Spirit. If you feel filled with the love and wonder of the universe, trusting yourself as a sovereign leader in your life, your energy body is strong and light. If you are holding lots of unresolved pain, afraid of what might happen next, and not sure where you fit or belong, your energy body is dense and dysfunctional. Obviously, we all have moments where we deviate between the two; the intention at hand is to be conscious of this deviation and address whatever issue/trauma/experience is blocking you.

Defining your relationship with your energy body is one of the first steps in a conscious spiritual practice, as well as a tool for moving out of your head and into awareness. Practicing this exercise strengthens the integrity of your boundaries, enhances your sensory perception, and helps you tune in to your guides and helping spirits.

Exercise: Energy body #1

Intention:

- Connecting with your sense of self
- Setting boundaries

> Find a quiet place to sit down where you will not be disturbed for 20 minutes. Be in a comfortable sitting position with your back straight. Hold your stone in your right hand.
>
> Close your eyes and take three long, slow, cleansing breaths, tuning inwards to explore where you sense your breath in your body. Do you feel it in your throat, ribs, shoulder blades, diaphragm, chest? Can you breathe all the way into your belly?
>
> See if you can use your awareness to deepen this breath until your whole being is filled with each inhale.
>
> Now bring your awareness to your heart centre, taking three breaths into this space. Think of one thing you love about yourself, maybe even say it out loud, and feed your awareness of this self-love to your whole being with each inhale and exhale. Notice what happens.
>
> Begin to imagine yourself as an orb of light. The edges of the orb are approximately two feet away from your physical body. Take a moment to engage all of your senses in this imagining. (Remember, it is fine to pretend; sometimes that is the first step to engaging actual sensation.)

Notice your orb's colour, texture, and density. It might glow, change colour, and even have its own frequency as you tune in to it.

Breathe in and out deeply as its full spectrum reveals itself to you three dimensionally.

Notice the boundary of your energy body. What is it made of? How permeable is it for taking in what you need while protecting you from what you do not? Do you need to make any adjustments? Take a moment to do so.

Now focus your awareness on the front of your energy body, scanning from head to toe and observing with all of your senses what is present. Take a full minute to relax into this as well as a full minute with each of the following:

- Send your awareness behind you, scanning from the top to bottom, taking your time and keeping your breath long and even.
- Now move to your left side, head to toe, breath by breath.
- And now move to your right side, head to toe, breath by breath.
- Are there differences from one side to the other?
- Send your awareness above you, two feet from your crown chakra. Notice, sense, and breathe.
- Send your awareness below you, beneath the floor or ground if necessary. Notice, sense and breathe.

Become aware of whether or not you are centred in your energy field. If not, what does this mean for you? Is it possible to adjust yourself so that you are?

Take three more deep breaths to sink even deeper into your awareness of your energy body.

When you feel complete, blow what you have learned into your stone with three strong exhales.

Begin to breathe yourself back to ordinary reality, breath by breath.

Take a moment to journal what you observed and experienced.

Do this practice daily until it becomes easy to summon this three-dimensional awareness in one breath.

Some variations include:

- Notice what happens to your orb when you expand to take up the whole space of the room or shrink as small as you can.
- Practice outside, a few feet from a tree. Tune in to your energy body and begin to sense the tree's energy body. What do you notice when the edges of your energy bodies touch?
- Try this practice with a friend. What do you notice about their energy body?
- What happens if you are conscious of your energy body in group settings? What changes?

CHAPTER 5:
Why We Don't Feel and Why We Need To

"But there was no need to be ashamed of tears, for tears bore witness that a man had the greatest of courage: the courage to suffer."

–Viktor E. Frankl, *Man's Search for Meaning*

There's an exercise I do in trauma healing workshops to help participants recognize the impact of blocked emotions in their bodies. It is usually on the second day, so people are comfortable enough with me and each other to start going a little deeper. I have each person identify emotions related to the specific trauma that we are working on, and see where they are holding those emotions in their body. Then they partner up. One person grabs a ball of yarn and wraps it three times around each part of the body their partner identified as the seat of an unexpressed emotion. Then, I have them walk around the room together. It is a visceral experience of engaging the felt sense of how they bind themselves and witness how others do it, too. There is the added realization that this binding exists energetically *all of the time* until the emotions are expressed. Thus, each person is walking through their lives wrapped in the invisible bondage of repressed emotions.

One year, there was a workshop participant who had almost every square inch of her body bound. She could not walk, even with the help of her partner, so she sat in the centre of the room—blind, as her eyes were bound, too. What the group did not know at the time is that she had stage-four breast cancer, and she knew she was dying. The grief and pain were everywhere inside of her, and she wanted to stop hiding it. In a private conversation with me prior to the exercise, she wondered if the group of fourteen women could hold the intensity of her suffering. My counsel was that she was there for herself and needed to show up for what was happening inside of her. She needed to tell her own story, and the yarn exercise was one of the many ways she was able to do so over the weekend.

To heal trauma, we must be our own barometer for emotional expression. We are called to trust what we feel, even when that feeling is different from what we *think* we should feel or what we assume *others* think we should feel. It is the heart, not the mind, that must lead the way to express what is within.

Emotions have no expiry date. They do not go away when unaddressed; instead, they fester and poison us. Feelings are energy that transforms through communication. Communication is a synonym in this instance for movement and expression. The tools are verbalizing, writing, physical movement, art, music, ceremony, or prayer. These acts propel you forward by drawing you deeper.

This is not easy for many of us. Particularly when trauma results in disembodiment, it is difficult to get back into your body to feel and heal the trauma. (The practices listed in Chapter 3 under "Getting into your body" are great assets for this.) With health issues, it is easy to feel like your body has betrayed you, and you realize that you have severed yourself from feeling what is happening within. Yet, like the workshop exercise above demonstrates, these emotions are still present. Ignoring them does not make it any easier to move through your life; in fact, it becomes more complicated as the mind seeks ways to remain disembodied.

To heal, it is necessary to examine what gets in the way of touching our emotional content. Here are a few common blocks to feeling.

My trauma is too big to feel

This shows up in two ways: it's too big to feel, period, or it is too big for you to feel in the company of others—to be seen in it. The latter was a common theme for me for many years. It was easy to think that my trauma would overwhelm those around me, so I should keep it to myself. I had many experiences where this was true. Murder is a definite conversation stopper, so I avoided talking about it. The few times I did became one of those moments where all other conversation around me stopped and everyone zeroed in on what I was saying—the good old "you could hear a pin drop" scenario. This level of exposure was way too much for me. It was easier to say nothing until enough time had passed and I needed to speak it out loud for *me*. I needed to feel it for *me*. (Fuck other people's reactions.) To go to the depths necessary for my healing journey, I had to express the violence of this loss.

If this is you, focus on the individuals in your life who can hold space for you to go there. If you do not know people like this, find them. Put the question into your daily practice by asking Spirit to help you locate the places, spaces, and people that will support you in moving to the next level.

If you are one who thinks your trauma is too big to feel at all, understand that you do not have to feel it all at once; it can be broken into less daunting components. Consider the conversation in Chapter 3 in "Approaching the Underworld": *you* get to determine what you need to feel safe in going there. This experience will be different from the original trauma. Take time to journey to the underworld and ask to see one piece that you can feel or manage for this day.

My trauma is too small to feel

This is akin to "Why bother? I've managed so far. So many people go through worse. I need to suck it up and move on." Remember, trauma is energy, energy is emotion, and emotions are energy in motion: they need expression, or they get stuck and you get stuck. If old wounds continually show up in your consciousness, they are asking for your attention. The victim self needs you to acknowledge that they are worthy and their feelings are valid. It is helpful to witness the emotions arising, and instead of making an analysis in your inner dialogue such as *-where do these come from and why am I feeling this-* validate them *-I am sorry you are feeling this way, even if I don't understand it. What do you need me to do to release or honour these feelings?*

A few years ago, I had a client whom I will call Avery. Avery came to many of my programs, but she could not find an explanation from her past to validate the inner conflict she was experiencing. Certain that she had no specific trauma, she felt she could not justify her emotional state. Her self-talk was, "Why do I feel this way? What's wrong with me? There is no good reason for this." This is such a common human theme: to negate emotions we perceive as illogical or nonsensical. Avery was overlooking compounded childhood experiences of neglect and abandonment from parental figures. These experiences reinforced her current feelings of unworthiness—of not warranting the necessary attention to heal. For Avery, healing meant letting go of the need to compare her pain to another's and acknowledging (not analyzing) what was present.

Trauma is contagious

When we share our trauma with therapists, friends, family, or even in workshops/circles that cannot hold the sacredness of our soul wounds, we can receive debilitating feedback or judgment. Initially this might shut you down; in time, it just makes you smarter about what you share, when, and with whom. People do not want what happened to you to happen to them. Their responses may feel like they are afraid of catching the infection of trauma that you have. They may carry an unspoken assumption that the victim is somehow to blame, and this can be made evident in the questions they ask. It's like they are looking for proof that you did something wrong (or, in my case, my mother did something wrong), so they can make sure they don't do whatever that wrong thing was and have the same thing happen to them.

Trauma is shameful

It is normal to feel shame and embarrassment regarding what happened and what this might mean, whether this is about us or another. As humans, we are meaning-making machines, and the assumptions we make in our heads define the reality we experience in our day. Do not let this shame stop you; it is simply a layer or a marker along the way. Instead own it, by going into it and expressing your experience of it. In fact, the shame itself often indicates the most important place to start. What is great about shame is the strong physical response that generally accompanies it. This gives you helpful information, such as where you have held the issue in your body and its relationship to your trauma.

Shame researcher Brené Brown has been instrumental in leading a global movement towards overriding the power shame holds over us. The following two quotes shed light on the necessity to heal our shame:

"Shame is the intensely painful feeling that we are unworthy of love and belonging."

"Shame derives its power from being unspeakable, if we begin to speak shame, it begins to wither."

– Brené Brown, PHD, LMSW

Disappointing others

Another common block around feelings is that we might disappoint others. Getting real with our feelings has consequences. Sometimes in our relationships, jobs, or family, we get stuck in a role that we no longer identify with, and to heal our trauma we must grow beyond the confines of this role. To be true to ourselves, we will disappoint others—and to move forward, we need to address this conflict.

This was huge for me, perhaps because I was only 20 when Mom died, and that is an age when we often begin to address issues with our parents. The emotional content that emerged in the years after her death went from initial love and adoration to the next layer: anger, judgment, and condemnation for how she had disappointed me, or had not been the person I wanted or needed her to be. Expressing these things— telling the truth about how I felt—required that I choose myself and how I was feeling over my fear of disappointing and betraying her. Just because she wasn't there in person didn't make this easier. In doing so, I was stepping out of the daughter role and into the role of an adult asking for accountability. Underneath that anger, I discovered my own shame and guilt for my lack of accountability in our relationship, and I was able to apologize for that, too.

Letting go of control

Feelings open us to the wild, sacred, feminine parts of our soul (even if you are male), and the fear of letting go of control can keep us from being willing to go into them. We do not know what will happen on the other side of feeling them. To surrender to our feelings, we need to be immeasurably present to the truth coming through us, letting go of the judgments that cut the process off. Crying and screaming like a banshee is messy, and there is a place for this in healing. Wailing at the side of a stream, pulling at your hair, and emitting guttural moans may also be part of the process. These aspects of crazy cannot be discounted. Trauma is crazy, and often we need to meet crazy with crazy along the way.

It reminds me of giving birth. I liked to call it the good old *hipshatteringpain* when I felt myself split open to bring forth life. If I resisted or tried to control the pain, I would not have been able to give birth. I had to allow myself to break open, to surrender to the force of chaos moving through me, go into the pain and let it teach me what I needed to do. Feelings related to trauma can be like this, where renewal exists on the other side of chaos.

The need to be strong

Our culture pays homage to the hero, and strength is valued as a commodity for success. We are inundated with this message through media, story, and film. Consider the emphasis placed on superheroes, war heroes, and other big, strong men. Though there is a place for warriorship, it needs to be balanced with its polarity: the ability to open, soften, and feel. Showing feelings is typically regarded as weakness. To feel means that the other guy—whoever this guy may be in our heads—will win, so we harden, ignore our feelings, and pretend that feeling is overrated.

The question to ask ourselves when this philosophy no longer works is, "What does it really mean to be strong?" When you suppress your feelings in the name of being strong, you may be pleasing who or what is around you, but you are waging an internal war that ultimately weakens you within and without. If the focus is on this emotive suppression, is it, in fact, strength? Alternatively, if you decide strength includes feeling and being seen in your vulnerability, then there is no internal war. It comes down to our decision to be true to ourselves.

Judging feelings as good or bad

We often have a binary approach to our emotions. We are willing to experience the ones we like, the ones that are acceptable and give us favourable sensations—you know, the "good" ones. The other fifty percent, the "bad" ones, are tucked away and emerge only when our daily decorum is challenged, and we are unable to keep up with false pretenses.

What if none of our emotions are bad, and it is only what we do or do not do with them that can be harmful? Each of us has a spectrum of emotions, ranging from violent rage to unconditional love, that may move through us within the course of a day—sometimes within the span of a few minutes. This is normal. And the more honest, transparent, and authentic you are with what arises within you, the easier it is for these energies to flow through and out. Rumi's poem, "The Guest House," is a beautiful example of this; look it up online.

Consider the segment above on disappointing others. For me, all sorts of emotions arose that could have been deemed negative or "bad." It would have been easy to think, "How could I say those things about my mother—that I hated her or that she abandoned me?" But the dark, negative emotions are part of the spectrum of feeling, and they, too, must be expressed. The fact is, once they are released in a healthy way, we are no longer bound by them. Once I told my mother the truth of these not-so-savory emotions, they were no longer one hundred percent true. More importantly, my heart opened to see my own part in the issue.

Journal questions: Feelings

- What blocks you from getting in touch with your emotions?
- What blocks you from expressing them?
- What emotions do you consider good?
- What emotions do you consider bad?
- How can you change the need to judge feelings and instead welcome their full range?
- Try a new form of expressing your emotions that makes you uncomfortable, and find out what happens when you do so.

Exercise: Energy body #2

Intention:

- Connecting to above and below
- Noticing where trauma is stored in the body

This exercise is centred on feeling your relationship with earth as Mother and all she sustains, as well as opening to Spirit. After you fill your energy body with your awareness of these relationships, you will practice identifying where you hold emotional blocks in your body. I recommend going slowly and fully engaging the felt sense with each of the components that are listed.

Also, when you are exhaling energy down, soften your pelvic floor muscles and feel your root as a filament of light moving downwards. When you inhale, tighten your pelvic floor muscles, literally pulling the energy of the earth below into your body.

***

Start by doing the first energy body exercise in Chapter 4 until you feel fully aware of your own presence.

> Once again, sit in a comfortable position, if possible, with your spine erect, holding your stone in right hand.
>
> Send your awareness to the bottom of your energy body and, on an exhale, imagine a filament of light moving from you into the earth below. This light gathers up the power of all that it touches. With each exhale, you send energy down; with each inhale, you pull energy up, filling your energy body as you do so…
>
> Imagine this root touches upon all that you love about the Mother Earth, expanding in an extensive network of roots as it moves down in each direction simultaneously…
>
> It touches the food which sustains you… Inhale, exhale and feel this connection…
>
> The waters that cleanse you… Inhale, exhale and feel this connection…
>
> The land that inspires you… Inhale, exhale and feel this connection…
>
> The energy that nourishes you… Inhale, exhale and feel this connection…
>
> Send this filament of light down deeper with each exhale until it touches the heart of the Mother Earth herself, connecting your heart to her heart, breath by breath.
>
> Draw this essence into every fibre of your being.
>
> Notice what changes in your energy body as you do this. What does this feel like?
>
> Next, bring your awareness to the top of your head and imagine you are sending a filament of light up into the Great Mystery. This light moves upwards and outwards as if you are the tree of life itself, spreading out in every direction simultaneously…
>
> This light gathers up the power of all that it touches—the power of Spirit—and you can breathe these connections into your energy body, filling you

with their strength. With each exhale you send energy up; with each inhale, you pull energy down.

You touch upon Grandmother moon… Inhale, exhale – feel this

Grandfather sun… Inhale, exhale – feel this

The starlight nations… Inhale, exhale – feel this

The cosmic galaxies of light… Inhale, exhale – feel this

You breathe in all you need to feel connected to the Great Mystery, touched by the Holy Spirit and open to the highest wisdom available to you. Grace, Divinity, and love are here.

Take three deep breaths in and out as you sit with this sensation.

Notice what changes in your energy body as you do this. What does this feel like?

Now call into your awareness the struggle you are having with trauma. Notice where you hold this conflict in your physical body. Take a few breaths as you inquire and observe.

How does this conflict impact your energy body? What has changed, and what does this mean?

What does this part of your body have to tell you about trauma? Listen to its story.

What emotions need to be expressed to release this block?

What is a healthy way for you to do this?

While you allow your answers to arise, remind yourself that if the content becomes overwhelming, you can pause and re-centre yourself, pulling energy up from the earth and down from the heavens as needed.

Blow what you are learning into your stone with three strong exhales.

When you feel complete, slowly breathe yourself back into the physical space you are in and take time to journal.

The freedom to feel

Our innate desire to grow naturally directs our attention towards healing trauma and its unexpressed emotions. We are born with an inherent internal wisdom that knows what to do and how to allow these emotions to move through us. They are kin to the creative life force. When given permission to move you, they will set you free.

CHAPTER 6:
Intuition and Fear

"The woods became darker and darker, and sticks cracked under her feet, frightening her. She reached down in the long deep pocket of her apron and there was the doll her dying mother had given her. And Vasalisa patted the doll in her pocket and said, "Just touching this doll, yes, I feel better."

– Clarissa Pinkola Estes, *Women Who Run with the Wolves*

"For the real change to take place, the body needs to learn that the danger has passed and to live in the reality of the present.

Our search to understand trauma has led us to think differently not only about the structure of the mind but also about the processes by which it heals."

–Bessel Van Der Kolk, MD, *The Body Keeps Score*

So far, we have taken the time to consider what we need in order to approach the underworld of our trauma, how the victim self needs tending, the awareness that emotions must be felt, and some common ways we shut them down. All these steps naturally bring up fear. The question at hand is: how do we navigate the fear that arises and learn to use our gut instincts to lead the way?

Once again, there is no map. We are using an animistic process that is based on direct revelation; you are the mystic of your journey. I cannot tell you how to do this for yourself. What I can do is offer stories and examples from my experience and practice.

Our gut instinct—our intuition—may be the most profound tool we have for conversations with Spirit and our spirit guides. Our ability to use our intuition is supported or hindered by how we meet fear in our lives. The key is learning to maintain a conscious relationship with Spirit, exploring our fear rather than allowing it to take over. In this chapter, we will work on learning to trust your gut, deal with triggers, face your fears, and not pass your fears on to your children.

Can I trust my gut?

Trusting your gut and trusting yourself go hand in hand. Can you trust yourself when you sense one thing and all outside forces say another? Can you validate the voice within over the voice without? Can you trust your gut more than the fear of what might happen? What energy motivates how you respond to your life?

Our relationship to trusting ourselves and listening to our intuition happens in the moment, which means we need to practice being present. Fear wants to drive us into the future of potential outcomes and situations beyond our control and respond to them *now*, even when they have not happened. Using your intuition to its fullest capacity means being aware of what you see, hear, smell, touch, and taste, and also what your energy body is telling you in the moment. Then you use your rational mind to differentiate between the idea of what might happen and what is actually happening. This is where you stop and notice if there truly is a lion on your tail chasing you down, or if you have gotten lost in an old story about a lion.

I found this to be a big struggle in the first few post-homicide years. The thing was, I knew my mother trusted her gut without a doubt—and then she was raped and murdered. She was the one who had instilled in me the mantra of, "Trust your gut, Sarah; pay attention and follow your instincts." So now, obviously, my mind wrestled deeply with this. Was her gut faulty? Was her intuition off that day, or was it simply time for her to go? My brain wanted evidence before I could trust again. It shouted at me that it was not safe to rely on intuition—it could kill me.

I did not know what was real anymore. For so many years, I had formulated my perspective on "If I believe I am safe, I am," and allowed my gut instincts to do the rest. This had protected me from harm when I lived a high-risk lifestyle in the downtown area of a large city in my late teens. But now, with my mother having been accosted in a dark place and unable to save herself, I knew I, too, could be attacked, raped, and murdered in a dark place, unable to save myself. Should I stay away from dark places? Expend my energy doing what I could to avoid potential rape/murder outcomes? Or trust my gut and hope it wasn't faulty?

The dilemma before me revolved around what I chose to do with what was present. The fact was, I could walk at night, and I might get murdered. Or I could never walk at night, and I still might get murdered. Trusting meant deciding how I wanted to live my life. Could I choose freedom despite this very real evidence of harm?

For me, trust meant stepping back from the chaos of fear and tuning in to what I knew at my centre to be true. Who I am—who we all are—cannot be harmed. This is something I've always known. It doesn't come from any particular spiritual or religious wisdom; it has just always felt like truth to me. That doesn't mean I haven't struggled with this concept or gotten caught up in fear in the past, but this knowing has been more dependable than deciding to live my life based on the possibility of death at the hands of another. We are infinite; what happens here is not the end of the story. This internal connection to Source energy—what I have referred to as Spirit—held more power within me than the fear did.

Journal questions: Instincts

- ▶ What gets in the way of trusting your instincts?
- ▶ What does your gut, your belly, feel like at this very moment? Take a second to notice. See if you can soften it with your breath; maybe place your hands upon it.
- ▶ Ask your gut, "How can I improve my ability to listen to you?"
- ▶ Ask your gut, "What do I need to know about facing fear in my life?"

Changing our response to triggers

To avoid being controlled by fear, we must learn about our triggers. Let us begin by considering what a trigger is and what being triggered means.

- A *trigger* is an external stimulus that may set off a fear-based response. For me, this would be entering a parkade, or a stranger following me while I am walking outside.
- *Being triggered* is your response to the trigger. Your response may be fear, or it may be something else.

These are two different things. A stranger walking behind me, day or night, is not bad, scary, or threatening. But my relationship to past trauma, if I have not processed it, may trigger me to interpret it that way.

Triggers are typically set off by sensory information that was present at the time of the trauma, such as sights, smells, sounds, or a sequence or pattern of events. For me, the sound of the music introducing a newscast, coupled with cold outdoor temperatures; the announcement of a current homicide investigation; or the smell of a certain brand of cigarettes can throw me back into the profound shock of my first year post-homicide. It can be one of those alone or a combination of them all; there is no way to accurately predict.

Trauma-based triggers can be debilitating. You *believe* what the fear is telling you. The inner dialogue may be, "Oh my god, I am back in this place again. I have no control. I have no power." Profound grief, panic attacks, anxiety, and the inability to breathe are common reactions. These triggered responses indicate that there is still grief, fear, and pain hanging out in your being, originating from your trauma. There is healing to do around acknowledging the victim, assuming personal authority, and expressing emotions, including fear. The question at hand is, how do you find that inner voice deep down in your belly to witness the fear before it consumes you? How do you know whether it is a real lion coming after you and threatening your survival, or just the fear of one?

Let me share a story to illustrate this process.

Overcoming a trigger

When I was sixteen, I was mugged while walking home one night. Walking alone in the dark, and strangers walking in the dark near me, became triggers. I knew I had ignored my instinct on the night of the mugging, which was shouting at me that I was not safe. My mind overrode that and said, "You are wrong, I am sure everything is fine," even when the person behind me started running towards me to rob me. Part of the reason I had ignored it, as ridiculous as this sounds, was because I had walked past the house of a guy I liked, and convinced myself that he had come outside and was the one walking behind me to surprise me. But I never turned to look.

I worked in the evenings and needed to support myself (I lived on my own), so I couldn't just avoid walking at night because of the mugging. Instead, I had to problem-solve what I would do if this situation arose again. The first thing in my control was changing my routes to more well-lit areas. Next, I needed to change my response when I sensed someone walking behind me. The reactive response in my head was screaming, "I am not safe, I need to run, get the fuck out of here!" But remember, it was my head that led me astray the night I was mugged. I needed to go beneath that energy to connect with the power in my belly, the knowing part of me, and be with what was present. This could be as simple as breathing into the moment and tuning into what each of my senses were actually interpreting. This practice generates an inner stillness that is deeper than the heightened energy of the mind in panic. It is an obvious difference and important to make note of. (Use the energy body practices in this book to support you with this.)

Once I tuned into the knowing part of me, other options became obvious. Instead of following my triggered panic response, I would either cross the street, slow my pace, turn and face them, or sometimes walk towards them. I even walked right up to a car that followed me home once and shamed the driver for his actions, standing my ground until he drove away. Listening to the wisdom within worked every time. It did not resolve the trigger, which is still present to this day, but it no longer controls my reactions. In time, as you decide to listen to your gut, you know when there is a lion and when there is not. This knowing is strengthened as it is exercised.

Intentionally facing your triggers

Taking action to face our triggers is like facing the monsters we believed lived under our beds when we were children. As a girl, I was determined they would not take me unawares, so I would search my room at bedtime and leave my closet door open so they couldn't surprise me. No corner was left uninspected—and I slept peacefully.

What we are afraid of leaches power from us. If we take time to identify our triggers, they have less chance of disarming us in day-to-day life. We need to look "under the bed" and in any other dark places we know our fear is most potent. If we combine this with the principles of approaching the underworld, we create circumstances that are more within our control, and our intuition is free to lead the way. As an example of this work, I will share how I faced two of my own triggers from the murder.

The parkade

The first trigger I had to face post-homicide was the parkade itself.

I had visited the parkade when Mom was missing, and on occasion throughout the first two years after her death. Those moments had been a big part of my mourning process. I would cry and sing "Amazing Grace" at the top of my lungs, and Mark, my then-fiancé, was always with me.

Now, I went alone, and my intention was different. This was in the third year after her death, when my grief was not so all-consuming, and I could question the details of her death with a little more ease. I now lived about ten blocks from the parkade, so when I found my legs moving in that direction on a sunny day, I felt safe enough to face this primary trigger.

I entered and paused right in the middle of the space. It was not that big—maybe room for sixteen cars—and there were never more than a few in there. I let myself go over the details of her death to see if they held power over me or if I had more mourning to do. I would recognize this through the feelings or information that came from my gut.

As my focus took in the whole space, I wondered if her earring was found *here* or *there*. What about her briefcase or the blood splatters? Was that the same car that was parked next to hers that day, the one that had a bloody handprint on it? For the life of me, I could not remember the make of that car. I'd look in the back corner, where it was assumed he had stood when she drove in, and check in to see how my body responded and what triggers came up. Did he move *here* or *there* when she tried to get out of her car? How had she tried to fight him off? My hope was that in facing this fear, I would gain some closure.

I let myself wonder what others thought or felt when they came into the parkade. There was still candle wax in the bricks along the outside wall, where the altars, candles, cards, and offerings had stood in the first year after her death. Did the people passing by sense anything? Did those parking here now know that my mother was likely killed right here on this spot?

I considered whether the parkade was haunted—if her spirit was stuck there—but it didn't feel like it. When I looked for her in that place, she was simply not present. All I felt in my gut was a cold, ground-level parkade with better lighting than it had on the day she died.

In those initial post-homicide years, my mind had turned the parkade into an entity of evil. This practice of immersing myself in it—a real-life journey into the underworld—helped me recognize the energy of fear and go beneath it to what was real. The parkade was not a portal of death or a place of evil, even though evil and death had happened there.

Walking at night

My second major fear was of a bad guy attacking me while walking at night. It was easy to recognize this fear because I had stopped walking at night, and I missed being outside under the moon.

I created a ritual to face this. At this point, it had been three years since Mom's death. The plan was to walk about ten blocks through my neighbourhood to the main street, which was only four blocks from the parkade. After walking on the main street for a few blocks, I would return through a residential area and then a big field before getting home. I felt connected to my spirit guides, had my German Shepherd puppy with me, and had told my fiancé my route.

My body was in a fear response the whole time. There were moments when I felt paralyzed and had to consciously coach myself and breathe. It was like I was in a police television drama: I'd either hide in the shadows cast by buildings and trees and look to see if it was safe before I made a move, or I'd be right up against the side of a building, peering around the corner. As ridiculous as it might sound, this fear was very real for me. My whole nervous system and physical body wanted me to run home, and I had to breathe through the impulse. There were many points on this walk where if I were attacked, there would be no one around to help me. My intuition, however, told me to trust, and that it would guide me. The resources I had at hand were my breath, my connection to Spirit, and the ability to make myself slow down rather than speed up. This act of slowing down actually tunes your senses in more to what is present and is a much greater asset for safety and survival than panic and fear.

When I arrived home, I felt like throwing up and dancing for joy simultaneously. It was a powerful initiation that forever changed the role fear plays in my life. I had demonstrated to myself that I had tools to override the triggered response of fear. The mental narrative of "OMG, someone will kill me if I walk alone at night," or "Being in the dark is dangerous and life threatening," didn't disappear entirely, but its power was diminished by creating a scenario that held similar elements and was under my control.

Journal questions: Triggers

- What trigger(s) hold power over you?
- What experiences created these triggers?
- What beliefs have you formed based on it?
- How are those beliefs impacting how you live your life?
- What support do you need to feel safe in addressing it?
- Placing your hands on your belly for a moment, ask yourself to feel the difference between an actual lion chasing you and your idea that there might be one. What do you notice?
- Create your own "real life" experience of moving into the underworld, similar to the two I shared above. Where do you need to go, what do you need to face, and how can you put together a situation within your control to empower you in moving forward?

Projecting fear onto our children

"Trauma not transformed, is trauma transmitted."

– *Tabitha Mpamira-Kagur, TedXOakland*

Sarah Salter-Kelly

How trauma impacts your fears for your children

When my twin girls were about two and a half, I had a profound fear of someone taking them. It was a feeling that can only be equated to cold, gripping terror. It became evident in my inner dialogue and influenced the activities I chose to partake in with them. I avoided crowds, events, and situations that held people we did not know, and it was becoming limiting. We needed to have conversations about stranger danger, and it was obvious to me that there was a fine line between educating them about simple life precautions and teaching them fear. I was contending with the giant monster of fear triggered by Mom's homicide and the reality I had experienced—that people can and will take your loved ones and kill them. Though I did not want my children to be bound by fear, it was difficult for me to teach them the basics (like not getting into a car with strangers) without coupling it with my terror—terror they could easily sense and feel. If I did not deal with this, I would be passing my trauma on to them.

The girls became fascinated with stranger danger. The idea that there were bad people who might take you was a curious mystery to them. Who were these people, where were they, and why would they do that—questions I did not necessarily have good answers for. I remember how valuable it had been in my own childhood to feel safe talking to my neighbours and say hi to everyone I saw when I walked to school. If my girls were afraid of their world, they would be disconnected from it.

I wanted them to trust themselves as I had learned to do—to get their answers intuitively, from inside of themselves, not outside, without being naïve or ignorant to the potential dangers in our world. What was happening instead was that my fear of losing them was overpowering sensible parenting. Often my techniques were governed by fear rather than wisdom.

Once again, I needed to recognize the difference between my own fear response and what my intuition was saying. I couldn't totally hear my intuition due to my profound vulnerability with these precious daughters. This meant I needed to better understand the energetics of the fear that was controlling me; then I could figure out how to diffuse its power and change my reaction.

Trauma as Medicine

Using the tools to face my fear

I used a shamanic journey to move into the underworld and find the soul-gripping terror of *What if I lose my children and there is nothing I can do to save them?* I saw that to release the power of this fear, I had to surrender to it being a possibility. In the safety of the underworld, I let myself imagine it. This could happen. I could lose my children and have no control over it. It wasn't likely, but it could happen nonetheless. I let myself feel the fear and grief of this. I also noticed an underlying layer of truth that I would never lose them, much in the same way that though my mother died, I know she is always with me.

Surrendering momentarily to the energy of potential loss reminded me that my power lies in the instincts gathered in the moment, not in the projections of fear from the mind. I knew that no matter what, I would do everything in my power to care for them and keep them safe. Doing my best and trusting myself was good enough; I did not need superhuman powers. Their potential life outcomes were far beyond my control, but I could put my energy into the values, ethics, and beliefs I wanted to give them as a foundation for seeing themselves and the world. That was what I could arm them with.

I also noticed that the connection between my role as mother and the loss of my mother played a strong part in my fear of losing them. I needed to let myself grieve and cry more in response to what was arising.

From that moment onwards, when we talked about strangers, I made sure I was present in my body and that what I was relaying came from my gut instinct, along with resources and tools to share with them. I could sense the energetic difference between teaching them awareness and imposing fear. I did my best to keep the fear out of it. I also educated them about the fact that strangers are simply people we don't know, and most are good people—but that the girls still needed to be with their Mom or Dad when talking to them.

Journal questions: Projecting fear onto others

- How has your outlook on life been cramped or contracted by your trauma?

- In what ways do you project fear-based philosophy onto your children or other loved ones?

- What physical signs does your belly/body give you when you are passing down a story of fear?

- Practice stopping and listening when you feel a fear response arising, rather than reacting to it. What happens? How can you change your patterned response?

Murder on the wind: facing the fear of what happened to our loved ones

There was a small part of me that always wondered if Mom was okay now, wherever she was. I was fairly sure she was, but I didn't have any evidence, and with the violence of her death, I was afraid that she might be lost, or worse yet, hurt in the great beyond. I really wanted proof from her and from Spirit. As the years passed and I sat with accepting her death, this desire felt like a crucial part of my own healing journey. Close to ten years post-homicide, this was the one little bit of energy still lurking that kept me from feeling at peace with losing her.

One afternoon, my prayers were answered with an unusual experience. I was standing outside on my driveway facing east when a great wind came upon me and swirled around me like mini tornado. Frozen to the spot with the power of its force, I began to sense my mother's spirit with me. In my imagination, she took me with her into the parkade and through the final moments of her life *as if they were happening to me*. I felt it all on fast forward in thirty seconds as the wind whirled and my hair blew around and dust settled. At the moment of her death, when she saw she was going to die, when she knew "this is it," a great wave of peace, grace, and light filled her. In fact, it is difficult to find words to describe what I saw and sensed, as I have never seen anything like it since. As she left her body, she transformed into a powerful light, radiating pure joy.

Awareness descended upon me, and I spoke out loud. "Oh, you are okay, you are showing me you are okay… thank you."

Feeling this as truth inside my own being was necessary to accept her loss. I still had not dealt with or faced her perpetrator, but this awareness cleared the way for me to do so.

Exercises and practices to strengthen intuition

Once you have developed a relationship with your energy body through the first two exercises, you are ready to try the following.

Exercise: Energy body #3

Intention: Learning your yes and no feelings

This is paramount to building a relationship with your intuition. Begin by engaging your energy body via the first two exercises.

> Call into your imagination the sense of something that you absolutely love. It can be a person, a practice, or a place on this planet. Fill your whole being with this sensation of love, calling forth each of your senses: smell, touch, taste, sight, sound. Name it out loud as you do so: "*Yes*, I love this." Let it move through your veins and activate each cell in your being with its energy. Feel the enthusiasm it elicits.
>
> YES. THIS.
>
> This is your **yes** feeling.
>
> Now clear, align, and neutralize your energy body.

> Call into your awareness something you do not like. Perhaps this is a type of food, mundane task, or a life experience you never want to have again. Pull it into all your senses: taste, scent, touch, sound and sight. Feel it coat your energy body inside and out. Notice how you respond on all levels to the essence of this.
>
> NO, not this—I hate this—No!
>
> This is your **no** feeling.

Knowing these two feelings as a felt sense creates a primary barometer for listening to your intuition. When you get the *yes* feeling, chances are you are being drawn towards something that is important for you. When you get the *no* feeling, it either means the definite *no* of a clear boundary, or that you are coming up against something you need to address, as you will see in the subsequent examples. Fear and triggers can be dressed up in the clothing of a *no* feeling, and there are times we need to check in and be with this sensation to determine which is which.

Exercise: Intuition #1

Intention: Develop your sense of knowing

> In this exercise, close your eyes and imagine yourself heading home. It is the regular route you take, and the path is familiar to you. Every detail is ingrained inside of you as the way to go home. You don't even have to pay attention, as your body knows how to get there. Notice the sense of knowing inside of you. There is a sense of self-assurance and unquestionable confidence. Perceive this sense of knowing with all your senses: smell, touch, taste, sight, and sound. You know where you are going, and you trust yourself to get there. This is your **sense of knowing**. It is related to your inner authority and works with the yes/no feeling to guide you.

Exercise: Intuition #2

Intention: Learn to adjust to obstacles on the path

> This time, close your eyes, feel yourself moving towards home, gather to you the sense of impenetrable confidence, and breathe it into your whole energy body. Now imagine that a roadblock appears before you, and the path that you normally take home is unavailable. Pause and notice your response to this awareness.
>
> Now find your connection to home inside of you. You know it still exists—home itself hasn't disappeared—only the way to get there has changed. Now you must use your yes/no feeling to discern which route to take. You do this by first feeling the sense of home within, moving towards the alternate route, and asking your inner guidance, left or right? Listen for the response: *yes, this way,* or *no, not that way.* Observe what this feels like.

Exercise: Intuition #3

Intention: Facing fear on the path

This is a great exercise for learning to recognize how you respond to unexpected triggers, as well as how to differentiate between the actual *no* feeling that means *no* and the *no* which arises in partnership with a fear.

> Close your eyes again. Pull yourself into the scenario of the second intuition exercise above, seeing yourself beginning to get comfortable navigating a new way home. You are learning to trust yourself and listen to these yes/no feelings for direction. Then something appears before you that triggers you. It represents an old fear from the past. Maybe you are driving into the darkness, and you cannot see where you are going. Maybe a person who hurt you appears before you. Whatever it is for you, notice your body's response. It might say initially, "No. Get the fuck out of here." Sit with it. Running away will not get rid of it. Breathe, and find that sense of home within. Ask yourself, "What do I need to feel safe *and* move through this fear?" Listen to

> the answer. Can you change your systematic response to this trigger? (This is not an actual lion; it is a story of a lion.) How can you problem-solve to continue on your route?

Exercise: Intuition #4

Intention: Understanding the ego's resistance to change

Differentiating between the *yes* and *no* feeling does not always feel clear for everyone. For example, let's say at the end of the day you start thinking about how great it would feel to have a regular meditation practice. You just know that you need to do this daily for fifteen minutes in the morning to release stress, improve health, and cultivate your inner resources. You are determined to follow through starting tomorrow morning. Your *yes* is vibrant, strong, and clear. You can visualize the result (let's compare this to the sense of home) and know this is right for you. (Once upon a time as a smoker, I did this most evenings: *tomorrow* would be a great day to quit.)

In the morning, you wake up from a tired and restless sleep. You remember you had promised yourself you would meditate, and this feels like a burden. That idea is added on to the list of everything else you need to do this morning, and you start to convince yourself that maybe it's not so important after all. Maybe you will start tomorrow. You check in with your gut instincts and it is a dead *no*. You knew it! You were not supposed to do it today after all.

Wrong.

This is one of the ways our *ego's resistance to change* sneaks in and hijacks or sabotages our intuitive impulses and personal growth. In the initial stages of change, our ego almost never wants us to do something that requires inner discipline. The secret in this scenario is to find the sense of home within. This is the metaphorical sensation of your long-term goal accomplished—the results of what the regular meditation practice will bring. When you pull this sensation into your body, it will give you a *yes* feeling. You are conjuring up a possibility of yourself that is vibrant and powerful. Now, the behaviours may initially bring on the *no*, as you are challenging yourself and changing the habits of your routine. Once it becomes part of a daily practice (typically, after at least 30 days), the ego's resistance lessens. This means that initially, you have to listen to the voice in your head tell you all the reasons why you don't have to do what you have committed to doing—and ignore it. Sometimes I pacify this voice with, "Thank you for sharing with me all the reasons why I can't, or the things I should be afraid of. I hear you, and I am going to give this a shot today anyway." Other times I am not so eloquent, and I just tell it to fuck off, asking the part of me that lives with conviction to lead the way.

> Practice this by imagining a scenario in your own life like the one I shared above—something you have wanted to add to your self-care regime or your spiritual practice for some time, but you get stuck in following through with it, even though you know you need it. Go through the steps of sensing this as a viable potential future you can feel in your body. Use all your senses to gather the information to you. "This is the feeling of me accomplishing this. This is what it smells like, tastes like, sounds like, looks like.... This is a real future reality. I can do this. YES!" Notice how this sensation changes the quality of your energy body. Sit with this for a few breaths.
>
> Next, make a 30-day commitment to follow through with this intention. In your practice, notice the voice of your ego as it attempts to override your intuitive awareness. Notice how it manipulates your self-talk or tries to make excuses that are contrary to what you want. See what happens when you observe this rather than engage it.

Making friends with fear

Learning to deal with fear means making friends with the unknown. Using all the tools we've discussed to listen to your gut instincts, you can recognize the qualities of your imagined lion and build a relationship with him or her. This lion is not here to eat you—it is here to reveal your current limitations and invite you to go beyond them. Find the courage to listen to the wisdom in your belly as you embark on this journey time and time again.

CHAPTER 7:
Metabolizing Trauma

"Evil (ignorance) is like a shadow—it has no real substance of its own, it is simply a lack of light. You cannot cause a shadow to disappear by trying to fight it, stamp on it, by railing against it, or any other form of emotional or physical resistance.

In order to cause a shadow to disappear, you must shine light on it."

–Shakti Gawain

In time, consciously tending to our grief and trauma naturally generates the process of metabolization. In biology, to *metabolize* refers to the chemistry of turning nutrients into new cells, energy, and waste products. What we're talking about here is very much the same: the process of digesting trauma into new growth and letting go of what we can no longer use. It's an essential step of healing.

Energy cords

To metabolize an experience of trauma requires two prominent steps and a whole bunch of little ones. First, we need to recognize where we store trauma in our body and follow the energy to what it represents. To do this, we will learn about energy cords. The second step is to do the work to be with, express, or resolve what has arisen through the awareness of the presenting cord. That's where the integration phase of healing happens: digestion and assimilation.

Metabolization calls for a deeper examination of what we are tied to or what we are in relationship with. The concept of energy cords is a viable resource for this understanding. We are tied by energetic cords to everyone and everything in our lives. These cords are comprised of our thoughts, feelings, and beliefs, and they connect us internally and externally to the universe at large.

The most prominent cords hold our strongest connections. Cords can connect us to people, to life-changing experiences, or to repetitive habits and patterns. In healthy relationships, these cords fill us with vital life force, and we share vital life force in return. In unhealthy relationships, energy is pulled from us, or unwanted energy is sent towards us, and we may do the same to others. Our job as conscious beings is to come into a harmonious state of reciprocity with all of our energy cords, taking responsibility for how we participate or engage with each connection.

Energy cords differ in weight, texture, colour, and viscosity, based on what they represent and how the individual perceives them. If we feel we are victim to circumstances (such as when I thought I was incapable of healing my mother's homicide and was stuck in the powerlessness of despair and fear), we are wrapped in dark, heavy cords. Our thoughts and fear feed those cords, and we are trapped within the dynamics of our own prison. It's easy to advocate for our own powerlessness; it's easy to say, "There is nothing I can do, look at what has happened to me." And this way of thinking, living, believing, and seeing simply continues to manifest in our inner and outer life experiences.

If, however, we choose to become conscious of each heavy cord and do our own work to resolve the issues inherent within them, we cultivate freedom.

We don't usually cut the cords we do not like. It is the same thing as avoiding conflict. It may be "easier" to avoid conflict, but it doesn't free us from *having* the conflict. To cut a cord, we have to do the work to be free of it.

Consider a relationship with an old friend who is unhealthy for you. You've decided to end the relationship, but have evaded voicing your reasons to them in person or on an energetic level. The cord connecting you to them is filled with the conflict of your unexpressed emotions. These emotions don't go away when the person does, and you can't eliminate the feelings by cutting the cord, because the conflict belongs to *you*. It contains energy you need to acknowledge, express, and resolve in order to heal and grow. They don't have to agree with you or be willing to hear, receive, or validate what you say. This is your work, not theirs. When you tend to this, you take care of this cord, freeing yourself of its bondage. Sometimes it unexpectedly renews the relationship as well.

We must integrate the teachings from the heavy energy and let go of what doesn't serve us. This is the act of metabolizing our suffering: digesting the experience, assimilating the nutrients, and composting the waste.

Our bodies store the emotional, mental, and spiritual information we encounter, and energy cords are connected to certain parts of our bodies. Think of how the shock and trauma of Mom's death hung out in my belly. In those first few years, each new piece of information went straight there. It also consumed my throat for many years. With these clues to how I stored the trauma in my body, I could follow the energy—a.k.a. the cord—between that part of my body and the experience. Then I could name and address it.

Finding the cords to trauma

An easy way to identify charged energy cords is through our triggers. Writing this book brought up many triggers for me. Reading old newspaper clippings or the notes from court drew me back into that time, instantly making me feel sick to my stomach and putting my nervous system on high alert. Likely this is why it took so many years to write! Each time I could ease back into the trauma differently, coaching myself.

"Sarah, you are not back in that time again. It is not happening now. Take a deep breath. You can do this." I had to send loving energy to the cord labelled *Mom's death* inside of me. And every time, even though it was anywhere from fifteen to twenty-four years later, I had to see if there was anything new I needed to be aware of or do to bring forth more healing. The worst trigger that came up during writing this book was the autopsy report, which I didn't read until May of 2017. It made me excruciatingly aware of the need to go deeper into the energy of murder. Whether it was Mom's death or murder in general, both were present in that cord, and they required all of my tools to address.

In the initial years after her death, I was like a ball of black yarn. Most of what I was connected to was painful. Piece by piece, this was unwound and resolved through being willing to approach the underworld time and time again, feeling what came up, acknowledging the victim self, assuming personal authority, facing fear, and working with acceptance. But it wasn't until I knew that Mom was okay via the "Murder on the Wind" experience that I could address the biggest cord of all.

I was connected to Peter Brighteyes by an energetic cord.

The Brighteyes cord

I had done everything I could not to think about him, which was actually a lot of work. He was dead, and according to the media, he'd had a difficult life, so I had not seen any point in expending my energy facing him—which meant I had not noticed the cord. I had numbed myself to the idea that it mattered. He was the face of my greatest fear and was really scary to think about, so naturally, in that first decade, I did all I could not to.

He haunted me anyway, coming into my mind unwarranted. I had no control over this, and I hated it. Typically, it was at the least desirable times, when my heart was wide open, like when I was about to make love with my husband or while I was nursing my babies. This immediately sabotaged the sense of intimacy and connection I was having. Instead, I was filled with a sinking, shameful feeling, and my mind focused on homicide rather than what was before me.

I tried everything I could think of to get rid of him, but the intensity and frequency just increased. At about the ten-year mark, I had had enough.

I was angry, touching a depth of emotion I had never been able to reach before. I had avoided feeling this anger even though I *knew* anger is always connected to power. If I was not expressing my anger, then I was not claiming my power.

I hadn't wanted to acknowledge that I could feel the same violence inside of me that had ended my mother's life. But once I gave myself permission to go there, there was no holding back. Rage welled up within me, and I wanted blood—his blood. How dare he get to kill Mom and have this power over me, too. It wasn't fair! I wanted to destroy him, to make him suffer like I suffered. The desire for vengeance and violence was palpable, primitive, and potent. I quite literally wanted to jump into my wolf body, tear Brighteyes apart, and eat him piece by piece. I knew I could trust my body to digest and metabolize his actions—to do what I consciously didn't know how to do—even if it was just on an energetic level. And if he was inside of me, he couldn't hurt me, sneak up on me, or haunt me when I least expected it.

I decided to get professional help, thinking another opinion would be of value. I knew it was a good thing that I was feeling him around me more and that my whole solar plexus was activated with anger. The psychologist I saw didn't see it this way. (Now, I did choose her by flipping the Yellow Pages really fast and sticking a pin in the section of psychologists to find her. Maybe this was not the best method.) Instead of initiating an experience to explore Brighteyes' proximity to me, she had the opposite approach, one you would expect from a fruffy New Ager, not a professional. She suggested I wrap him in pink light and see him slowly disappearing. When I said that this wasn't strong enough for me, she told me to imagine him slowly floating away in a hot air balloon. I didn't bother telling her I wanted to eat him. Likely she would have prescribed medication.

What I have learned through my years as a healer is that you can only take people as far as you have gone yourself. This woman just couldn't go there. This did not mean I couldn't go there on my own, which is a crucial element in the story.

If I had listened to her, even when my whole body was screaming, "This is wrong," Brighteyes would have continued to haunt me. It would have taken me longer to figure out how to heal this, as I would have been debilitated by her point of view—which is easy to do when you are being advised by someone who appears to be an expert. You need to claim sovereignty over your own process at *all* times, only taking in external feedback that aligns with your own sense of knowing. (Those are great times to do the intuition exercises.)

When I got home from that appointment, I was filled with a momentary sense of helplessness as to what I would do next. Then a wave of knowing came over me and I stopped myself with these words: "Sarah, you have power! Do something about this yourself! Stop waiting for an expert; there isn't one." I knew that my awareness of this cord was a game-changer. If we were connected, I was not powerless or at his mercy; I could intentionally call his spirit in.

Creating my own ceremony

I had never called in or held a ceremony with someone who was dead before, and I wondered how to do it. Was it dangerous? I mean, he *was* a murderer. Was there a specific technique? I couldn't find any information on this in any books, and I didn't have the internet as a resource. (Yes, imagine that: way back in 2006, not everyone was cyber-connected.) What would I have typed in the search box, anyway, "Express anger towards spirit of man who killed your mother"? or "How to speak to spirit of dead man"?

There was no script.

What I *did* know in my heart of hearts was how to create sacred space, set intention with prayer, and listen to Spirit. This was part of my regular practice, and it had been for almost fifteen years. I decided to trust that and use my understanding of ceremony as a tool to directly address this cord. I could commit to finding time once or twice a week, when my twins were in kindergarten and my son was napping. That gave me two hours per ceremony. I often joke that I have great time-management skills, and if there's a will, there's always a way.

This ceremony began in January of 2006 and ended in November. The only consistent structure was setting up an altar, invoking sacred space through prayer, welcoming my spirit guides, lighting a fire, smudging and purification, and calling in Brighteyes' spirit. My gut told me that I had to hold each ceremony in alignment with my understanding of the five directions and the five elements, beginning with the east. (At the time, my practice included five directions: east/spring/air, south/summer/fire, west/fall/water, north/winter/earth, self/inner/akasha.)

This meant I spent about two months in each of the directions, applying their cyclical teachings to what I was learning and to my intention. Once the space was created, I listened and responded according to what I sensed from my guides or what my heart told me needed to be expressed. A lot of this was acknowledging being victimized by him and how that impacted my life. My inner warrior had refused to do this before; I had never directly blamed him, and now I needed to do this out loud. I had spoken *at* him before, back when I was trying to get rid of him. Now I wanted him to *hear* me; I wanted to speak *with* him. I screamed, shouted, drummed, sang, journeyed, wrote letters, and burned them. I let the wild chaos of my inner banshee rise up within me to name my horror and how wrong his actions were. My core intention was the cultivation of personal freedom, so I had to be willing to look at everything that got in the way. I felt confident in how Spirit was leading me and had no attachment to the outcome, other than the desire for freedom.

It was a lengthy and painful process to find all the unresolved energy in my body, identify its cord, and tune in to what I needed to do with this information. However, I had no time limit. I had already held this energy for over ten years, and I was committed to however long and whatever it took to finally release it.

Before I began these ceremonies, I didn't necessarily believe that a spirit would come if you called it. But from the very first ceremony, I felt him near, and as the ceremonies progressed, this sense became more and more intimate—uncomfortably so.

The journey that changed my life

Each time I went into that ceremony, Grandmother Bone Womyn, my helping spirit, would be there to guide me. One day, two months into the ceremony, Grandmother Bone Womyn led me to lie down and go on a journey. In this journey, I had a vision that changed my life forever.

This is what I saw:

> I am sitting on a sand wall in a desert landscape. My feet can touch the ground, and the wall I sit on is about two feet wide. Before me is a pathway that leads to a small pyramid, maybe four stories high. Intuitively, I know it is a holy place, a temple of this land I am in. The sun is shining down upon me, and I am covered in a long wrap to keep off its glare. My left arm sits in my lap, while my right arm is draped around a boy who sits with me. He is

> about nine or ten, and I am pulling him to me in a loving embrace the way you would your own child, teasing him, and sharing a close camaraderie.
>
> He is troubled by something that he has done, and he knows the time is fast approaching when he will have to take ownership for it. It seems to me that he will have to go to this temple before us. I comfort him with my arm and my words, assuring him that there is nothing to be afraid of and he needs to take responsibility for his wrongs. This well of love fills me and wraps around him in the way that is only possible for a mother to soothe her child. Compassion and understanding motivate me to encourage him. "Go now, you can do it."

My conscious mind suddenly kicked in and pulled me out of that journey, with a loud, *"What the fuck was that?"* I knew that the woman was me, and the boy was Brighteyes, and I knew—I felt it, for God's sake—that I had just had a profound sense of compassion for him. How the hell was this possible? He was a murderer! How could he be deserving of compassion?

I was in absolute shock. This wasn't what I wanted. I felt pissed off, like my ceremony had somehow been hijacked. I was doing this to finally express my anger, not to feel love and connection!

It made me even more angry as I realized the feeling wouldn't go away. I could not shake it, and it left me confused and overwhelmed. Brighteyes was the source of the greatest pain in my life. How could I possibly feel even one iota of love towards him?

I decided the best thing to do was to let these feelings sit until I could make sense of them—to digest them. I didn't feel like the ceremony was complete, and I was determined not to stop just because I had this life-altering revelation. My mind needed time to catch up to my heart and integrate this experience. So I continued each week, wanting to make sure I was thorough in listening to and expressing my feelings through each of the five directions, so that I went full circle.

During this time, there was a great weight around me, like a thick black cloud, as I held space between the worlds. I couldn't speak about what was coming up for me or what happened during each ceremony, as I didn't understand it all myself. Plus, I knew that if I attempted to give words to the sacred nature of my experience, it would lose its power. The words themselves would disintegrate the meaning of what I was encountering, as what I was learning still belonged in non-ordinary reality, not in this one. My husband knew a little, and he cautioned me to take care of myself. Some days I could feel myself stretched out as a living bridge between reality and spirit.

One night in March or April, something really strange happened as I was going to sleep. I was lying in my bed with my eyes still open, and I saw a semi-circle of Grandfathers in front of me, waiting to get my attention. Instinctively, I knew they were a Council of Justice from the beyond—a circle of Elders. Peter Brighteyes stood in front of them. He was in chains, and he was looking directly at me.

They spoke in unison. "You need to forgive him." I swept the air before me with my left arm, and they disappeared. "*No*," I screamed in my head. "I am not ready yet."

Listening to Wolf medicine

I hadn't been able to shake the image I'd had of stepping into my wolf body and eating him. It came up regularly, despite the new-found experience of compassion. It was confusing to sit with such duality: compassion versus the desire to tear someone apart. There was not one or the other in me; there was both.

I wanted to listen to my instincts and create a ceremony to follow through with this, but I was initially stumped by the ethics. *Do no harm* is practically welded into my core make-up, and I needed to know if this would be okay. Could a person do something like that without causing any harm? Would it be wrong to visualize this? Would I hurt him? Are you allowed to eat a spirit? I didn't have the answers.

My instincts have always led me in the right direction, but at that moment, I doubted their credibility. Was there a line between visualizing intent to harm and causing harm? I had always thought they were one and the same. But I also knew I was tired of feeling like prey, and the idea of stepping into my wolf body changed that dynamic entirely.

What I needed to do was metabolize murder. This meant taking back my power and not being victimized by his role as a perpetrator in my life. Surely I could do this in sacred space in a way that was in balance with all my relations. What I was learning in these acts of ceremony was that my relationship to him was already internal, and as such, I had the power to do something about it. This idea of *eating* him through a journey gave me a visual image for what was already true—that he was inside of me—and I could step out of feeling like a victim, a.k.a. prey.

Another way of looking at what this was like for me comes from a teaching I received from the Q'ero nation of Peru. Following this ceremony, I spent many years learning from them. They are highly regarded as masters of energy medicine. They view all energy in terms of its potential refinement, believing there is no such thing as good or bad energy. There is simply heavy energy, known as *hoocha*, and pure, refined energy, known as *sami*. Most experiences and people, and even some places, contain both. Only humans produce hoocha, and it is transformed into a higher quality of energy when we digest and metabolize it. There are exercises in Andean Shamanism that teach you how to do this; you energetically pull the hoocha into your belly centre and take the time needed to process it. This can be a few hours or years, depending on what you are transforming. I had pulled the hoocha from my Brighteyes cord into my belly consciously, and Wolf simply wanted to give me a visceral experience to metaphorically represent what was transpiring. The heaviest hoocha—the shit produced through digestion—would go to the earth as compost: the hate, anger, shame, or blame. The nutrients, the sami, would fill my being in the act of metabolization. Compassion had already shown up. This philosophy is right on par with what I orchestrated myself in the following Wolf ceremony.

One morning (about six months into the ceremony and four since the experience with compassion) I followed my instincts at last. Stepping into my wolf body was not new for me. Wolf has been a consistent spirit guide since I was eighteen years old. Back then, I often went out to play under the full moon in the forests and meadows of the downtown core, which were in fact the golf course or the river valley. I would sit in the grass where city met wilderness and let my body become one with Wolf. Looking out over the stretches of green, I'd use these wolf senses to evaluate the environment before me and determine my safety before I made a move, making sure there were no predators nearby so I could move into the open under the moon. So now, in the comfort of my living room, it was easy to visualize shifting into the body of this close spirit guide.

I physically got down on the rug on all fours. There was a sensation of ears tuned in to deep listening, a nose that could find anything, and fur covering my whole body. The bulk of my strength was in the force of my upper haunches, and I could feel every hair, all the way to the tip of my tail. I imagined myself tracking him, reversing the roles of predator and prey so that I was the predator. A surge of energy filled me, until the moment I had been instinctually drawn to for over six months came to pass. I imagined eating him, and in this act, I reclaimed my power. He couldn't hurt me or haunt me anymore, and I didn't need to worry about him showing up unexpectedly in an intimate moment, because I was no longer afraid.

In fact, after this ceremony, he was so close to me energetically that he was with me all the time, whether I liked it or not. I was, after all, metabolizing him. It became so intimate that I could smell him, taste him, and feel his breath. I was letting myself stomach who he was and what he had done, taking time to be with it. I couldn't predict or name at that time what this process was transforming into; that would have pulled me out of the felt sense. Instead, I felt each dark emotion, impulse, or reaction, and I sat with them until they changed. Eventually, no new ones arose, and that indicated I was ready to complete the ceremony.

In November of 2006, ten months after I had begun, I held a fire ceremony to mark its ending. I actually saw him approach the fire from the North, dressed in full First Nations regalia—the first time I had ever seen him look empowered. We parted ways at the fire, and I saw him walk towards the Southwest. That was the official ending of my ceremony, though it was not the end of my work with Brighteyes.

Digestion

It took me years to digest this. As I worked through the process, I continued to journal, pray, and ask, with my hands on my belly, "What do I need to learn? What can I let go of or release? What can I assimilate as nutrients to grow stronger? Which components in this cord are transformative, and which are not?"

I could not deny that I now felt a shared sense of humanity with Brighteyes inside my heart (where I *really* didn't want him). But it was true. I saw that he was not different from me. For years, I had only thought of him as a bad man who killed my mother. Now I knew he was not worth less than I was because of what he did. His spirit/soul has equal value to mine.

This did not change or excuse his actions in the least. He was and will always be responsible for what he did to my mother. But there was more to who he was than one act of murder. He was also a human being.

This was puzzling for me. As I inquired inwards, I saw that I held a belief that one's worth is measured by one's actions. The fact that his soul and mine could be on equal ground challenged this belief. I found myself stepping out of the personal nature of my pain and starting to contemplate the greater picture, which led to the next step on my healing journey. This inquiry was a mark of the metabolization process going on in me, as I was starting to ponder what nutrients I was assimilating from Mom's homicide. I had let go of my need to hate or condemn Peter.

Journal questions: Metabolization

- Who or what is haunting you?
- What are you avoiding or pushing away, and why?
- Placing your hands on your belly, notice the weight of this issue.
- Ask your belly, "What must I do to metabolize this issue? What must I digest and release into compost, and what must I assimilate as nutrients to sustain me?"

Ceremony: Addressing a person who has done you wrong

Tools: The stone you have been using through this book; journal, smudge, and musical instruments, if you choose.

Time: About an hour

- Set up an altar specifically for this ceremony. Consider what you need to feel safe in facing someone who has done you wrong, (review Approaching the Underworld) and find elements that symbolize this to place on your altar. Trust your intuition.

- Smudge and cleanse yourself and your altar.

- Have your stone in your right hand.

- Create sacred space (see Appendix for my version, or use your own).

- State your intention: Be clear about who is haunting you and what you want to address. Perhaps notice what energy or emotions have been coming up that you know need to be moved and expressed to pinpoint your intention. For example, mine was an overall desire for freedom and to address anything that was unexpressed in relation to Brighteyes, primarily my anger.

- Tune into your energy body. Take a few minutes with this so you are grounded and centered.

- Ask where you hold the energy relating to this person in your body. With a few centered inhales and exhales, gather information about this energy. Become aware of the cord that connects you to this person. When you are clear, call this person into the space formally, using their full name.

- Next, notice all the heavy, unexpressed energy in this cord. What have you never given voice to? If you could say *anything* now, what would it be? Feel the energy you are awakening inside of you and listen to what it needs. Does the victim self need to express her trauma in a new way? What is present for you?

- Content (at least 30 minutes). *This must be organic to your process.* How will you express this energy? You can drum, dance, scream, sing, cry, do nothing and just be with it, write it down, do a shamanic journey, ask your spirit guides for help, or track it further in your body.
- When you are complete, blow what you have learned about this cord into your stone with three strong exhales.
- Place your hands on your belly and sit with yourself, taking deep breaths, until you feel complete.
- Close the sacred space.
- Smudge yourself and your room.

Care for your stone. It holds the energetics of what you are addressing in this cord, as well as the other processes in this book. Treat it as a sacred object.

Do this ceremony in increments, listening to your nervous system so that you are taking in or expressing out what is manageable day by day. Remember, I did this twice a week over the course of almost ten months. Take your time. If you get overwhelmed, engage your energy body and fill yourself with the essence of above and below. Alternately, go on a journey to your place of power and simply lay on the ground to recharge. Take as much time as possible to be in nature, for this is the most important place that can ground you and cleanse your body, mind, and spirit.

As for the wolf ceremony, it is one that I lead in group or through private mentorship. Contact me for details.

The value of indigestion

Metabolization is not an overnight affair. In fact, the older I get, the more I see that we revisit it at different stages and ages in our lives. For no matter what we do to heal, the wheel of life turns again, and we revisit significant events and experiences in a new way. Knowing we are sustainable beings who are able to process what has arisen gives us the confidence to face our discomfort and the moments when we inevitably must delve once again into the underworld. No matter what we do, we cannot escape indigestion—the sensation our body uses to get our attention and tell us that something needs to be taken care of.

For me, these cords presented in layers. Initially, I was so wound up in the energy of trauma that I could not get to the cord that represented Peter until ten years had passed. As you read above, once I named it, my intention directed my experience. All of the components listed in Chapter 3 had to be in place before I could feel safe and secure in facing him. I tended the victim, assumed my own power and authority, expressed emotions, and faced my fear. Then I stopped, listened, and allowed Spirit to guide me. I was also in conversation with my mother all the time, who was coaching me with her New Age mantras and encouraging me to do this.

What became evident as this energy was expressed and digested was a profound well of compassion and an understanding of shared humanity. This is what I was assimilating. To use the terms from the Q'ero in Peru, this was sami, the pure white light energy. The hoocha—the need to hate, hurt, or see Peter only as a despicable human being who was worthless—became the compost I gave back to Mother Earth.

When I finished the ceremony ten months after it had begun, the cord was clear. I could feel that when I checked in to my energy body. It hadn't gone away, but it was clear. There was the sensation that there was nothing left I was responsible for, so I simply put up a stronger boundary towards this cord and said, "We are done."

The most important takeaway I hope you receive from this chapter is that you *can* metabolize your trauma, and in time, it will bear elements that transform you.

CHAPTER 8:
The Teachings of Forgiveness

> "So when I am asked whether some people are beyond forgiveness, my answer is no. My heart has been broken a thousand times over at the cruelty and suffering I have seen human beings unjustly and mercilessly inflict upon one another.
>
> Yet still I know and believe forgiveness is always called for, and reconciliation is always possible."
>
> –Archbishop Desmond Tutu, *The Book of Forgiving*

At the time of her death, my mother had the following affirmation on her bedroom mirror:

> I forgive myself
>
> I forgive everyone
>
> I am free

The power of her words was not lost on me. I mean come on, what are the chances of a woman who was brutally murdered having such a straightforward affirmation about forgiveness on her mirror?

Forgiveness had not been anywhere on my radar until after the ceremony with Brighteyes. Before that, my grief process took precedence over his role in what had happened. To examine forgiveness too early would have felt like he was being given greater importance than the very real loss of my mother and the violence of how it all went down. Instead, I began to contemplate it organically as an obvious part of metabolization in due time.

My thoughts naturally started to turn towards wondering what forgiveness was and what it meant to me. It's easy to slap forgiveness on top of pain without it being embodied or authentic. It is easy to say, "I forgive you," and not live it or practice it. I needed to know what *real* forgiveness was—for *me*.

Initially, I was concerned that if I forgave him, he would get to keep a part of me that did not belong to him. Or that he had won. Or that I was saying what he did was okay. Would forgiving him be a betrayal to Mom? Obviously, given her keen love of forgiveness, this would not be the case, but it came up in my inquiry nonetheless.

After I had expressed all of my anger and pent-up emotions towards him, it was easier to ponder forgiveness. I came to see that forgiveness meant I was no longer blaming him or holding him responsible for what had happened in *my* life.

I went back and forth with these ideas for a time. Then, in the fall of 2007, I was in a shamanic training program. We were doing a process outside that related to honouring our teachers. I had gathered stones, flowers, sticks, and other natural objects to create a mandala that would represent this. Each item had been intuitively gathered without attaching a name or a face to it. I walked the land, asked my guides how many objects I needed and which ones would work, and gathered them in a good way. (This meant asking permission from the land, leaving offerings in exchange for what I had collected, and inquiring as to how I could give back in order to be in balance.) At the moment of use, I would intuit who and what each item represented.

I had gone through my pile, naming which teacher each object related to in turn, such as my folks and other mentors who had played a starring role in my life, and I blew my connection into each of the objects with three strong exhales.

Initially, there were no big surprises. Then I came to my last object. As soon as I picked it up, a profound revelation dawned on me. Peter Brighteyes was one of my greatest teachers.

It was such an exceptional, unexpected awareness. Shivers and tears surfaced as the truth of this moved through me.

I knew it was time to forgive him; to do so would honour the teachings steadily coming into my life, the ones indicative of metabolization. Obviously, I was not grateful that I had lost my mother, or that he had killed her. But by being willing to look at this loss to deepen my understanding of who I am, I had come to a place where forgiveness was an option, and I was grateful for that.

It was important for me to forgive without trying to make the heinous act of violence he committed okay in any way. I did not try and pretty it up, consider it an accident, or make any excuse for his actions. I needed to forgive "as is."

I first spoke the words "I forgive you, Peter" out loud nearly twelve years after Mom's death, in the fall of 2007, in front of that mandala—interestingly enough, in the Peace Country of Alberta, nor far from where she was born.

After this experience, something completely unexpected happened.

Peter Brighteyes became my spirit guide.

It was almost instantaneous. The next day at the same workshop, I saw him approach me. He was warning me about someone who did not have my best interest in mind. I was so angry that he was there, I did not get the message at first. I was like, *"What the hell else do I need to do here? I found compassion, expressed my feelings, and forgave you, oh my god, go away!"*

However, he was insistent that I listen, so I did. In that particular case, this meant becoming aware of an assistant to the teacher, who was mis-using his authority towards me. I had been totally naïve, assuming that spiritual people were beyond jealous or vindictive reactions. I had lots to learn, and Peter's warning that day helped.

His guidance became more and more consistent over the next few years. I would see/feel him near me, and each time he would warn me about something or offer accurate insight. I had to remember that I had asked the highest powers of the universe for the best possible outcome. That meant I needed to be open to what was showing up, not try to control it. And what was showing up was the spirit of the guy who killed my Mom as a helping spirit. As weird as this was, after a few months of disgruntlement, I accepted his help.

Healing synchronicity

I wrote about the experience of compassion and forgiveness in *The Mosaic*, a local body, mind, and spirit magazine. When the magazines were ready for pickup, I drove to the city, excited to see it in print. When I arrived, I realized that the shop was on the same street as the parkade where Mom died—in fact, less than ten blocks away. As soon as I opened the magazine and saw the article, I knew I had to go down to the parkade and create a ceremony for her.

The parkade itself had changed somewhat since that fateful morning in December of 1995. It had an actual garage door that locked now, so I could not go inside. I tuned in to my higher guidance to question what I was supposed to do here, and I could see that I needed to pull the article out of its bindings, roll it up, tie it with hair from my own head, place a stone in it, and put it in the opening between bricks.

I questioned my guidance when I saw the image of the hair. (*Really, a piece of my hair? That's a little creepy.*) However, my inner guidance had a good track record, so I did as I was told. When I brought it to the wall, I stretched my hand out to touch those bricks... bricks that had held many altars for Mom through the years. Bricks that held together the building where she took her last breath. Bricks that laid the foundation for me being there at this moment in time. "It's done, Mom," I whispered. "I have done this for you—all of those crazy ideas you had about healing, about anything being possible. All the ways your spirit marked me and led me are here now in the words on this page, an offering to you and to whoever is led to read it. May it bring light... may it help us to heal... I love you."

Eight months later, I was contacted by a woman who found the article in the bricks. Here are her words.

> Dear Sarah,
>
> My name is Amber. I am writing you regarding an article you wrote. Eight months ago, while my Auntie Becky and I were driving to her apartment, we saw what we thought was a wallet on the side of the road. After we parked, we walked over, and it turned out to be a leather biker's cap. During Easter of 2003 I tragically lost my mother; Becky lost her sister. I am convinced that she was murdered by the men she lived with, who were bikers. I have a lot of anger towards these men. My life has been consumed with fear, anger, and hate. I was obsessed with not knowing the whole truth of how she died. I told Becky to throw the hat away, as it reminded me of my loss. I feel the angels were at work as Becky instead carried it with her, towards her apartment. There was a parkade with a brick wall on the main level of the building facing the street. As I turned my head towards it, I saw a piece of paper rolled up and tucked into the wall. I picked it up, slightly hesitant as it was wrapped in hair. As I began to unwrap it, a rock fell to the ground. Becky and I looked at each other, feeling like we were meant to read it. We slowly unrolled it and read your story of healing over the murder of your mother. I went through waves of emotions as we read it—I was sad, I cried, and then I got angry. I did not want to hear it all, particularly the part about choosing our deaths (even murder) and finding forgiveness for a murderer. Becky looked at the biker's cap in her hand, then at me. "You know what I think this means," she said. "I think this means we have to forgive him." At the time, I was mad at her for even considering that. In the last few months, I now see that this is the only way I may truly heal. Your story has given me so much. I am deeply grateful to have been the one to come across it. It was meant to be.
>
> God bless
>
> Amber

A copy of Ambers letter first appeared in an article I wrote "Forgiving Murder" in Mosaic Body Mind and Spirit Magazine, Winter 2010 issue. Found online at https://mosaicmagazine.ca/forgiving-murder/

Journal questions: Forgiveness

- What has happened to you that you deem unforgiveable?
- Notice where it hangs out in your body and what that feels like. Describe it on a sensory level. For example, connect with the sensation of **unforgiveable**, notice the issue it is related to, and feel where it is located in your body. "I feel it in my right hip. It is sharp, pointy, electric, smells like sulfur, sounds like deep moaning, tastes like gas, looks like piles of thistle..." Get as descriptive and symbolic as possible; the more imaginative the conjuring, the better.
- What energy cord(s) is it connected to?
- What must you understand within yourself to make room for forgiveness?
- What needs to be released and resolved?
- What teachings may it bring into your life?

Ceremony: Forgiveness mandala

What is needed: a relatively private place to sit outside that you can return to over the course of a week/month.

Tools: smudge, offerings (see Appendix), journal, pen.

Time frame: an hour or two.

Smudge.

- Tune in to your energy body, ground and centre.
- Open sacred space.

- State your intention out loud: to create a mandala out of objects in nature that represent what forgiveness means to you, including who you need to forgive.
- Place offerings on the land, stating your intention and asking permission to gather objects to support your process. Ask to be guided to find the right ones for you. Ask how you can give back in order to be in balance.
- Find objects from nature such as sticks, leaves, wildflowers, rocks, shells, etc. These objects are to represent the following, and there can be more than one object for each:
  » Boundaries
  » Helping spirits/guides
  » Your trauma
  » Who is connected to the trauma
  » Who you need to forgive
  » Why you feel you can/can't
  » What forgiveness means to you
- Sit down. Using these objects, make a picture or a mandala on the ground, letting your creativity, imagination, and intuition lead you. There is no right or wrong way to do this, let yourself explore what feels good for you. Each object you place into the mandala must be named out loud and have its essence blown into it. For example, say, "This represents my mother," then bring the object up to your mouth, touching it directly to your lips and blowing into it.
- When the picture/mandala is done, sit and observe it for at least 30 minutes.
- Notice the symbolism in what you have created. What does it mean to you? What do you need to know about this? What does forgiveness have to say to you? What is the relationship between each of the objects you have placed on the ground? How do you feel about your boundaries? What surprises you? Where are you stuck? What can you change? If

> necessary, rearrange objects to be a more accurate representation of what you are noticing. Observe again.
>
> - Journal.
> - Close sacred space.

Take time to return to this mandala over the course of a week or a month. Each time you sit down, tune into your energy body first. Then notice what your mandala feels like and what has changed. Is there anything you need to add or change within it? Take your time to do so. Is there anything that nature or Spirit has added to it of their own volition? Take a moment to observe and notice what this means to you. When you have developed a greater understanding of forgiveness, you are ready to dismantle the mandala. Do so with love, giving thanks for what you have learned, and return the objects to nature so that you leave no trace.

CHAPTER 9:
Ayahuasca and Trauma

"First you must confront yourself and all that
you fear to see that you are nature, you are not
separate; your relationship is symbiotic.

Ayahuasca takes you there, connecting with everything
that has ever been suppressed or forgotten."

–Don Luis Culquitón, Ayahuascero

I simply could not compose a book about trauma and the underworld without touching upon the medicine of Ayahuasca.

A vine found in the far reaches of the Amazon, Ayahuasca's popularity has risen in the past decade as a viable tool for healing trauma, disease, and addiction. Used medicinally by indigenous people since ancient times, Ayahuasca is known as a master healer, and is referred to as *Grandmother, vine of the soul,* or *vine of the dead*. She gives you a direct encounter with the mythos of your wounds by initiating hallucinogenic visions that stimulate your felt sense. These visions relate to what you fear, what is unhealed, and what you have repressed: the undigested aspects of your life. She compels the body to purge (literally vomit) the toxins caused by this unresolved suffering and assimilate the grace revealed.

Hallucinogenic plant medicines or chemical compounds are not new to westerners. The recreational use of psilocybin, LSD, and MDMA are common among spiritual seekers. Psilocybin and LSD were essential teachers in my own journey, primarily between the ages of sixteen and eighteen. They gave me an understanding of myself as an energetic light being and the sensation of being connected to Spirit. They taught me the necessity of acknowledging and facing fear. These teachings happened far from an intentional spiritual ceremony; I used them at clubs, house parties, and occasionally in nature. But even though my early psychedelic trips were not focused on receiving a spiritual lesson or having a sacred experience, it always happened anyway. They gave me a foundation for understanding myself and Spirit that was fundamental in addressing Mom's homicide. Coupled with my training in altered states, such as shamanic journey, naturally I was curious about Ayahuasca. If spiritual revelations arose without intentional ceremony, I wondered what transformation was possible if done with intention. This story would not be complete without a journey to the Amazon, and an introduction to how plant medicine in the form of Ayahuasca can help us heal trauma.

Sacred intent and power

What makes Ayahuasca unique (and different from a recreational high) is the intention to connect with the sacred and heal ourselves. In so many parts of our world, ceremonies sourced from relationship with plants and the land disappeared with the dominance of organized religion and the push of colonization. Likely because the Amazonian people live in such remote locations, their relationship with Ayahuasca has remained strong. Though the method and technique of working with her varies according to tribe and medicine person, there are foundational components that remain the same. Their common thread is to show you that your connection with God comes from within.

Unlike a typical spiritual practice that requires the discipline of regular meditation, inner work, and journeying, Ayahuasca transports you into an altered state—often at the speed of light—with no need for prior experience or training. This has its pros and cons. I have noticed through my years of working with Ayahuasca that when she is approached with respect and reverence as a sentient being, the results are vast. When she is approached with expectations of a prescribed outcome, the demand for an immediate solution or transformation, or without engaging in one's capacity to participate and do their own work, there is often much more struggle (purging) in the process and the experience is not as clear. She cannot be controlled or dominated, as much as our minds try. Working with her involves surrender.

It is important to note that I am not an expert on Ayahuasca. I have been to the Amazon on five occasions between 2009 and 2015, twice as a group participant and three times bringing my own groups. It is my sense that I would need to work with her for decades to really know her, and even then, I would not be an expert. What I share with you comes from my personal experiences, what I noticed in my group participants' healing, and what I learned from working with and interviewing the Ayahuascero (Medicine Man) I worked with on each occasion.

Taking Ayahuasca in the Amazon

Location matters. Spiritual experience can happen anywhere, but there is something to be said for taking the time, energy, and money to make a pilgrimage to the Amazon. This is not a trip for the faint at heart, for the Amazon is primitive and extreme. It is hot, humid, messy, and muddy. There is an insurmountable quantity of bugs, who will get into your bed, clothes, and nose. You will get bitten. At the Kapitari Sanctuary, which is where I went for four of the five trips, the accommodations were extremely primitive: no running water (until 2015, when communal showers were set up in a common area), limited electricity (and none in the cabins), no cell service, and toilets flushed by pouring a bucket of water into them. Never mind what might end up in the toilet or bucket—mine had a giant frog hiding under the rim of the toilet bowl once. Nothing against frogs at all, but it's kind of hard to sit down and go when you see something alive looking back at you from the bowl.

Regardless of all this, there is a wild soul that exists in the heart of all the inconvenience and discomfort. Reflected by the luminescent wings of the giant blue morpho butterfly, this a place where magic is born. Everything within you automatically slows down and tunes in to the present moment… to the sensation of sun on skin as you feel the heat of day, or water on skin as you move through jungle ponds or rivers. The sounds of the insects in the evening is like a symphony, their pitch and harmonics written simply for your listening pleasure, with intricate changes in their vibration and frequency. The Amazon is thought to be the lungs of the planet, and these lungs ask you to breathe deeply of your relationship to life, to Mother Earth, the Pachamama and Mamacocha, the Mother of the waters. You cannot extract the power of Ayahuasca medicine from the Amazon. And though many people participate in these ceremonies in the western world, there is a natural power generated when you drink the brew where it grows.

What is the Ayahuasca brew?

The vine is combined with the plant *chakruna* and cooked over an open fire from twelve hours to a few days, until the mixture is reduced many times and a medicine brew is formed. This mixture contains DMT—also known these days as the Spirit Molecule—which is believed to create new neural pathways in the mind that change our habitual response to suffering.

Ayahuasca ceremony

Your ceremony begins the moment you commit to working with Ayahuasca, regardless of how far in the future the ceremony is planned. I am not kidding. There is a palpable shift in your life as she reaches back from your future encounter and starts to show you how to prepare for her seismic impact on your life. There is, of course, a diet; you forgo all stimulants, sugar, alcohol, and salt (along with a list of many other things) for at least six weeks prior to ceremony. This flushes out the everyday physical toxins, making it easier for her to address the older, more latent issues stored in your body. Remember, the energy of all life experiences—emotional, mental, physical, and spiritual—are stored in the physical body, and Ayahuasca works on all levels. Cleansing with diet ahead of time makes a huge difference in her ability to be more specific with your core wounds once you are in ceremony. I observed this repeatedly with participants who ignored the diet and those who did not.

Trauma as Medicine

My preference as a facilitator and a participant is to spread the five or so ceremonies over the course of two weeks, giving ample time to be with what is unfolding.

The ceremony itself is held in a round building called a *maloca*, which has a conical roof made of leaves, and walls constructed of mosquito netting. On the floor, places are set for each participant: a yoga mat, a blanket, a bucket, and some toilet paper (to wipe your mouth). The medicine man is called an Ayahuascero, (male) or Ayahuascera (female). My Ayahuascero was Don Luis, and he had an alter set up beside his seat that held, along with other tools, the medicine brew; a little wooden bowl for group to drink the brew from; *mapacho* (ceremonial tobacco); a *shakappa* (a rattle made out of leaves); Agua de Florida and other floral waters, used for cleansing; and Palo Santos, an Amazonian smudge for protection and purification.

On the day of ceremony, no food is eaten after 1 p.m., and a bath is taken in specially prepared floral waters, outside, naked, with little privacy. The afternoon is spent in meditation in the quiet of each person's *tambo* (cabin), listening to the ever-present sounds of the Amazon. Around 7 p.m., the group gathers in the maloca and chooses a mat to lie on; there might be anywhere from ten to thirty people in the ceremony. I often went early with my group to do a check-in circle, a meditation, and a smudge. It gets dark fast in the Amazon, and there is one candle lit in the centre of the maloca. To begin, Don Luis offers a prayer, and then the light is extinguished. One by one, people go and sit before him to drink the Ayahuasca. He says a prayer for each person, blowing tobacco smoke on the them and the brew.

Then Don Luis begins to sing his *icaros*. These are ancient medicine songs that have been given to him by the plants and his ancestors to support people's healing with Ayahuasca. After about a half-hour, people begin to purge. This is different for everyone, and the first ceremony is gentler than the second or third. Generally, the icaros guide you within yourself, where you have visions of the underworld relating to your fear and how you typically manage it. Visions of your death. Visions of your soul wounds. You are seeing the symbolism of the energy connected to any or all of your present day issues, which of course is often tied to the past, and purging it. Sometimes people fight the urge to purge (this is pretty common for westerners), but then the experience becomes about observing your need to control your body and learning you have to surrender at some point. It will, after all, come out the other end eventually.

After a few hours, Don Luis comes around and does a personal prayer, a tobacco smudge, and he sings icaros over each person. Once he has blessed everyone, he closes the space with a prayer. The whole experience takes anywhere from three to seven hours, depending on the group and what healing is unfolding. Some people choose to stay in the maloca, and others make their way to their tambo. The ceremony often continues for each individual throughout the dreamtime and into the next day. It is a time of deep connection.

An interview with an Ayahuascero

During my second visit to the Amazon in 2010, I interviewed Don Luis. Living a few miles outside Iquitos on the opposite side of the Nanay River, he has served his community all his life. In 1980, he founded Kapitari, an organization and research centre dedicated to protecting and preserving the biodiversity of the Amazon. The money he makes through ceremonies and teachings is given back to his people by funding projects that educate local farmers on permaculture and sustainable agriculture. At the time of this writing (2020), he is in his early 70s. The following interview was translated by Ryder Sandoval.

Sarah: Tell me, Don Luis, how were you trained in the medicine of Ayahuasca?

Don Luis: I was born Don Luis Culquitón in the village of Manacamiri of the Cocama tribe outside of Iquitos, Peru. When I was seventeen years old, I moved into the jungle and made my own hut. I was guided by God and my Grandmother to go there. The energy of nature called out to me. I could hear plants talking, and I understood. I could help people that doctors could not help. My icaros were taught to me there by the plants, and some by my late grandmother; there is no difference between being dead or alive.

Sarah: How would you describe Ayahuasca to one who has never heard of it?

Don Luis: Ayahuasca is a master plant containing the DNA of the universe. It is a female plant, and it is combined with another, called chacruna, that is male—perfect balance. Ayahuasca is a plant of investigation. You discover through vision which species of plants will cure your ailments. First you must confront yourself and all that you fear to see that you are nature; you are not separate. Your relationship is symbiotic. Ayahuasca takes you there, connecting with everything that has ever been suppressed or forgotten.

Sarah: How is it best for one to prepare for an experience with Ayahuasca?

Don Luis: It is very important to have a proper diet for six weeks ahead of time—no sugar, no salt, no sex, no alcohol—to realize that Ayahuasca begins to teach you before you arrive and to be grateful for what teachings come to you as you prepare for your journey.

Sarah: You have spoken a few times about how important preparation is for the person; how about the preparation for the plant? What are you thinking about while you prepare?

Don Luis: I meditate, calling to the plant and its medicine from as soon as I pick it and during the twelve hours of cooking it. I always offer tobacco for the plant. This is important to ensure good medicine.

Sarah: How do you create sacred space in the beginning of the ceremony?

Don Luis: Cleanse and welcome in God and the jungle. I use the shakapa (leaves that sound like a rattle). They are like a bell at Mass to call everyone in. Then I use them again at the end to call in nature and offer gratitude.

Sarah: Why do you blow tobacco on each of us at the beginning and end of the ceremony?

Don Luis: To synchronize your energy. It helps to open and close the ceremony in a good way. Tobacco into the heart and the brain to connect the two—otherwise you leave this place with no brain and no heart... (laughs). It also protects you.

Sarah: Each time I have been a part of the ceremony, I am in awe by the sense of God that fills me. Why does this happen with this medicine?

Don Luis: We are all God. Ayahuasca helps you to remember.

Sarah: Many people are coming to Peru looking for a cure for cancer. In your mind, what is cancer and how can Ayahuasca be of benefit to those seeking help?

Don Luis: Cancer is energy motivated by personal or genetic imbalance. It is catalyzed through imagination, GMOs, toxins, and anger. The mind creates all our sicknesses. Ayahuasca helps to purge the body of the sick parts of the mind. I help to motivate the person to release, to vomit out these dark patterns, and then I find the plants that will help to heal their body. It is best for them to do most of the work themselves; when they see their own darkness, Ayahuasca shows them they can cure themselves.

Sarah: What about for those who are coming to address trauma?

Don Luis: The mind holds dark energy patterns of the trauma. Ayahuasca shows this to them; as they purge and release, she shows them they can heal themselves. Therefore, she is a master plant.

Sarah: What do you think of those who are attracted to using Ayahuasca as a drug?

Don Luis: They come to get a new drug and then they see it is not like that. It is not addictive, and it shows them that they have God inside. In fact, it heals addiction. This is good.

Sarah: Many are learning of Ayahuasca and cannot make the trip here to the Amazon. How do you feel about ceremonies being held outside of the jungle?

Don Luis: I want to share this with the world. Here is better, though. There are some who may be mixing it with other plants, which can be dangerous; without creating sacred space, it is risky.

Sarah: Is there a final message you would like to impart?

Don Luis: I look after my people. I want to continue to care for those of my community, to share with a new generation. Through sharing Ayahuasca medicine with westerners and bringing them to the jungle, they learn about what an integral ecosystem we have, and in turn they may shed light on sustainable ways to protect it and the people who inhabit it.

My experience

The first time I worked with Ayahuasca was the spring of 2009. It was in the height of the H1N1 pandemic, which I had scarcely acknowledged prior to getting on my plane in Canada. I got stuck in Mexico City, as Peru was not accepting flights from Mexico, and I had to fly to Santiago, Chile. I was determined to get to Peru. Even if I had to hitch a ride up the coast and cross over land, I was going to do anything to get there. When Don Luis says the preparation begins ahead of time, he could not be more on the mark. I confronted so many challenges before I was even within a hundred miles of the Amazon. My trip was scheduled with a group that was to spend two weeks in the high Andes, camping and exploring the temples of the Sacred Valley, and then one week in the Amazon. Because of my delay, the others were three days ahead of me, camped somewhere on the Apu (sacred mountain) of Ausangate. To find them, I had to go from sea level to over fifteen thousand feet up a mountain in less than ten hours, fighting off altitude sickness. I was led by a guide I hired at the last minute, who barely spoke English and was not convinced we would find them. It took a day and a half to do it, but I did. Each event along the way taught me about my resilience and capacity to do anything I put my mind to.

By the time I was in the Amazon, I did not feel afraid. I welcomed the sounds of the forest and the land, as well as the primitive locale. My intention was to deepen my spiritual training and tune in to anything I needed to heal that I was not presently aware of. It was about a year and half since I had formally forgiven Peter, and I wanted to check in to see if I had missed anything.

The first night of ceremony, I did not trust Don Luis or his helpers. They gave me no reason to feel this way; I had just heard too much information about shamans misusing their power, and I needed to be sure it was a safe place to let go.

The dosage I had was gentle enough that most of my experience consisted of feeling the frequency/vibration of the sounds the numerous jungle insects make. They wrapped around me like a blanket. I felt like I was *becoming* the sound, like it was informing me of a new pattern of being where I could merge with its existence and let go. I laid down to visions of bugs eating me, causing slow, repetitive deaths. I wanted Ayahuasca to bring it on, to take me as deep as possible and show me everything I needed to learn. The walk back to my tambo that night in the dark on the jungle path, with only a small kerosene lamp to light the way, added to the etheric quality of moving into the unknown.

The second night, I had an entirely different experience. (This was the night I referenced in Chapter 3, where I had a conversation with Jesus.) Certain that I had not had enough Ayahuasca the first time around, I went up for more after about an hour. Don Luis smiled at me and asked me in Spanish if I was sure I needed more. I replied that yes, I did. He told me that sometimes, more is not always the more you think it will be. I understood enough Spanish to understand him and implored that I was sure I needed more, and that more would be the right more for me. He conceded, blessed the brew, and I drank.

Within an hour of the second helping, I felt completely paralyzed and at the mercy of relentless visions of death, shifting to machine-like worlds that acted symbiotically with certain songs that were sung. I had to remind myself that I was not actually paralyzed, and I could get up to purge or have a sip of water. This was a struggle, to say the least. There was one song in particular that went right to my belly, stirring up my need to purge and showing me more of these machine-like worlds (which I hated, as I wanted to see something different). They were the mechanics of my mind, my ego's need to hold on to how I form reality. I fought this and had a hard time letting go. At one moment, I thought to myself, *"What the hell were you thinking, Sarah? Coming all the way to the Amazon to work with Ayahuasca. You are frozen to the ground, high as a kite like an acid trip gone wrong, unable to move—and you think this is healing? And you paid a lot of money for this! This is crazy!"*

When it was my turn to go up to the front and be cleansed that night, I could barely walk. I sat on the ground in front of Don Luis, and he cleansed each of my energy centres with tobacco smoke. Then he began to sing an icaros right over my head, shaking his shakappa on top of my head and down my back to cleanse me while he sang. His voice opened like a doorway, and I saw all his ancestors singing through him. In the intonation of song and movement of rattle, I saw the spirits of the Amazon singing through him, sharing their medicine. I felt held by the power of this, and it disarmed me. Any remnants of ego protection slid off me through the floorboards to the earth below. It was a moment I recall vividly as one in which I allowed myself to receive healing, prayer, and support.

What came that evening, and in the other ceremonies in the Amazon through the years, was a deep connection with the All, the oneness of creation, what I name Spirit—*as long as* I learned not to follow the trajectories that were habitually launched by my ego to keep me distracted from letting go. In fact, often what I would be shown in the beginning parts of the ceremony was a manifestation of the unhealthy patterns my mind conjured in its desire to feel important or to be someone. Going deeper into the ceremony required me to release this need and trust what was undeniably present: my soul self.

What I noticed on that first Amazon trip in reference to Mom's homicide is that the continual grief work I did in my day-to-day life was working. Mom came to me in each of my ceremonies, and I was shown a place I call the Medicine Lands, where it is easiest to sit with her.

As for Peter, I saw that the wolf ceremony I did where I ate him was in direct correlation with the work of Ayahuasca, as she shows you that what you fear is in your body, particularly your belly. She teaches the need to purge the toxins and assimilate the gifts—like the concept of metabolization. It is also the same philosophy as energetic cords. You are connected to—in relationship with—all that has transpired in your life. There is no getting away from this. Ayahuasca is a teacher who pulls you into a direct, personal confrontation.

At the end of the ceremony, when the struggle is finished and you surrender to the medicine, there is a great stillness or peace. I believe this is, in fact, *always* present; we are just too busy to notice. One of my greatest takeaways from Grandmother Ayahuasca is this peace, this knowing that when I stop my busy, meandering mind, Spirit is here. Peace is here.

Your experience

If a you are called to use Ayahuasca or other plant medicine in your healing journey, you will know by how they show up in your mind's eye or in the conversations of those around you; this is how they talk to you. You will be attracted to her and curious about her. Books about Ayahuasca will appear, or people will share stories from their experiences. You might have a strong desire to go to the Amazon. That is one of the foremost indications of the need to build a relationship. Alternately, you might have a strong aversion. If you want absolutely nothing to do with her, that, too, can indicate the need to form a relationship. If you are neutral, then likely she is not for you. Use your intuition. There are many reputable Ayahuasca centres; do your research. Often those with more rules and structure are a good place to start. Find one that has a history of working with westerners and some understanding of the cultural differences. Ensure that there is a daily circle to help facilitate what has shown up for you. I encourage you to commit to at least a fourteen-day journey, with time and space between ceremonies to be with yourself.

It is important to note that you are a collaborative participant in your journey with plant medicine. It is not a process that is happening *to* you. The more intention you place on honouring these plants as sentient beings who are sharing their consciousness with you, the more your heart will open and connect with what you need to heal.

PART III:

Gathering the Bones

CHAPTER 10:
Finding Our Shared Humanity

> "Rather than delineate perpetrators and victims, sacred and profane, physical and metaphysical, the feminine welcomes everyone to the table.
>
> Like the Great Mother herself, the feminine mystic does not view creation as a damaged object in need of repair, but rather as a beloved child in need of care. Effective activism arises from unconditional love."
>
> –Mirabai Starr, *Wild Mercy*

> "People can and must come together with a willingness to share rather than to fight, to transform trauma rather than to propagate it."
>
> –Peter Levine, *Waking the Tiger*

We are not separate from the wounds of the world. Collective healing is the art of considering this larger picture. It means you recognize that what impacts you, as personal as it is, also has an energetic source and an impact on the issues being played out in our world—and therefore can be a part of its healing.

In Part I, I led you through the darkest underworld of my story to give you a visceral example of trauma, and I supplied a context for what I would cover in Part II. My intention was to use words, stories, and examples to support you in naming and claiming the truth of what has unfolded in your own underworld. Using the techniques of Part II, I hope you can identify and implement the acts of resolution required for personal transformation and healing.

For many, that is enough. The processes support you in defining the boundaries of your healing journey and allow for wholehearted integration. There is a sense of completion and peace, and you acquire the knowledge and experience needed to face any recurring issues or triggers. You share what you have learned with those you love and the world around you through the art of daily embodiment. This is beautiful.

Other people's journeys are not yet complete. Compelled by the need to participate in an intentional shift in global consciousness, these people cannot stop. There is an innate drive to understand the root of human suffering and use themselves as a tool to effect change. They struggle with big questions: Why does violence happen? What compels people to hurt one another? How can I do something about it?

Neither type of journey has more value than the other. They are both rich with purpose and meaning, and it is not my intention to imply preference. We all have reasons for being here and must follow our internal guidance.

However, it turns out that in this scenario, I am the type of person who could not stop at forgiveness. I needed to find the answer to *why*. I was driven to do anything I could to prevent other people from losing their mothers in such a horrendous way. I had to understand the bigger picture. This search sent me into another stage of the journey: collective healing.

As I begin to lead you through this piece of my story, it is my hope that all of you—even those who have already reached their end point—will still sit with me and listen. For those of you who are called to pursue collective healing, I hope it will serve as a rudimentary road map and provide encouragement. This is a story about shared humanity, and it carries teachings applicable for all of us.

Trauma as Medicine

Walking in the shoes of the other

One of my favourite quotes is attributed to Archbishop Desmond Tutu, and goes something like this:

> "My humanity is bound up to yours, for
> we can only be human together."

It is based on the idea that we humans are one: everything I do affects others, and everything you do affects me, and everything we do, together or apart, ripples out and has an impact on the whole of humanity.

Peter's actions changed my life. I needed to walk in his shoes to know him and imagine what it must have felt like to have the life he had—a life that led him to that moment where he met my mother in the parkade. I had to let go of any pretense that I was better than him because I was not a murderer. If I hadn't let that go, I could not really have walked in his shoes. This is an essential part in learning how to see the other. Given the right set of circumstances, I, too, could have been a rapist, murderer, or abuser. This act of imagination—to walk in his shoes—had to be totally clear of any judgment or condemnation.

Of course, this did not excuse what happened, but it allowed me to understand that many factors came together to result in his wrongdoing.

I knew almost nothing about Peter's family in 2010; all I knew about his lifestyle was that it was mired in addiction, trauma, and institutionalization. It was easy for me to assume that he did not feel connected in this world and that he must have undergone extreme circumstances to become so violent.

The truth is, for someone to defile, demean, and degrade another to the point that they take this person's life, they have likely been at the receiving end of defilement and degradation. A significant act of violence does not randomly occur one day. It probably has roots in past experiences of feeling diminished and unlovable, and likely of being harmed by those in power, whether that be authority figures, parents, or a racist society. We know that hurt kids hurt kids, and they grow up to be wounded adults who hurt adults.

Once again, I wondered if Peter was doing the best he could with what he knew at the time—even when that response was to kill.

Societal trauma

There were two significant elements in my mother's homicide that were hardly mentioned at the time of her death: race and gender. This murder was an intentional act by a First Nations man towards a white woman. Despite this, race as a contributing factor was barely acknowledged in the newspaper coverage or in conversations I had with family and friends. Intuitively, I knew it mattered.

In 2007, I was just learning that colonization in Canada hadn't ended a hundred years prior, as I had thought. In fact, it can easily be argued that it is still present. I started to recognize that despite how liberal and open-minded I thought I was, to some extent, I still viewed First Nations people through the stereotypes and ideology that had been fed to me by the overculture. (*Overculture* is the dominant culture in a society, whose mores, traditions, and customs are those normally followed in public.) I needed to look beneath these societal messages to learn the truth.

As I researched the history of Canada and started to unveil the real story in relation to First Nations, I became aware of my ignorance. My perspective came from indoctrination and white privilege. I was astounded to discover that the last residential school closed in the 1990s. This was not a long-ago issue. This was in my lifetime. This was *now*.

I could not help but wonder what response is needed in our present society to make amends for the shameful history I was discovering. I wondered if our inability as a society to acknowledge this responsibility contributed to my mother's death. In my heart, I needed to know what I could do to change this.

Unfurling the seeds of compassion

In the summer of 2010, before a sacred fire in Eugene, Oregon, on a starlit summer's eve, I was given a profound initiation that propelled the next part of my journey. It could be said that I gave birth to compassion by letting myself feel the depths of my own pain and that of the world. It was a moment where I was given an experience and a vision that meant there was no going back.

At that time, I had been formally training in shamanism and energy healing for four years under a few teachers. I was assisting in a program with one of them when the event in question came to pass. I had enough practice and experience in the energetics of ceremony to trust in my relationship with Spirit and to know I could surrender to what needed to come through me.

Seven days into the program, the class of about fourteen was sitting outside around the fire after supper, preparing to go on a shamanic journey. Ironically, the intention of the facilitator was to guide the group in an experience of compassion through meeting Kwan Yin.

I had had a few unsettling events that day, and found myself in a powerful, unexpected grief response. Embarrassed that I might disturb the group's process and uncomfortable being seen in such vulnerability, I tucked myself off to the side of the circle near a supportive friend. I could turn away from the group there to be with the sobbing that was becoming more and more uncontrollable by the minute.

I had met this friend, imani White, just a few days prior (imani has requested that her name is not capitalized). It was one of those connections where you feel like you've known each other for ages. She is a ceremonial musician, healer, and medicine woman, and when I sat beside her, she knew I needed help. She put her hands on certain points on my spine and chest that opened me to more grief flowing through—a river of tears, snot, vomit, and all. She did not try to stop me, fix it, or change it in any shape or form; she just held space and intuitively found more places on my body to touch gently, instigating an immense outpouring of emotion.

This went on for over an hour. Grief became water, became wave, until whatever had triggered my initial response was no longer relevant. I was grieving for everything and everyone. All of the pain and suffering of humanity was moving through my body, pulsing from each of the four directions simultaneously. It was paralyzing. It looked like rivers of energy from each quarter that moved down through my crown chakra, which I then expressed through my visceral emotive response. I was oblivious to the fact that the group was done with their journey. I couldn't pay attention to anything other than what was moving through me.

imani asked me to stand and face the fire. Initially, I could not. Unravelling my body from my safe spot was too much to manage. And I so desperately did not want to be seen in this grief. However, the intensity was not waning. Though I had no concept of time, in reality, it had now been over two hours. Because

I felt safe with imani and trusted her leadership, I relinquished any remaining sense of control or propriety and listened to her.

She placed a ceremonial staff in my hands and had two women help support me, as I was too weak to stand on my own, and then she had me face the fire and the group. When I raised my gaze above the flames, I faced a circle around me—about ten people—and felt enveloped by community. On a personal level, this was a really big deal, to be seen in such a raw state, no longer hiding or worrying about what anyone thought, but opening and allowing. It also represented the collective necessity for grief to be held by community, and my spirit knew this instinctively. The energy flowing through me amplified and began to transition from the mess of grief and trauma to deep wails of compassion and grace.

The change was palpable on a physical level. My body wanted to bear down, to push this energy through me. Waves of contractions overcame me.

imani prayed and sang aloud. Her hang drum carried prayers to the heavens and blessed me with the significance of this moment. The sole gentleman present was asked to be the water bearer. He fetched water, and imani poured it over me with more prayers and encouragement to drink and listen to Sprit.

The sobs had their own pulse, their own beat, synchronizing with the sounds around me. Their intention became more and more focused as my body asked me to bear down. The odd rational thought that popped into my head, such as "What are you doing?!" couldn't compete with the power of this energy. I looked up and saw the bright light of Venus, and I felt a primal knowing that my body was opening for life to come through. I had physically given birth twice before, and I knew exactly what it felt like. I looked at imani as my legs convulsed in contractions and said, "I can't stand any more. I am going to give birth."

I was lowered to my knees, my thighs vibrating, and the pace of the contractions increased, their intonation and climax culminating with the energy of my efforts. As I pushed, I became the portal where heaven and earth meet, where birth and death meet, where sorrow and compassion are one—the universe flowing through me in an act of transmutation. Where the chaos of our greatest suffering is grieved and felt, it is transformed into new life.

Through my body's travail, I was the Mother Goddess, birthing the energy of compassion that is sourced in the transformation of trauma. imani asked me, "What have you given birth to?" and my response was, "My Mother," as in the Divine Mother archetype.

I felt this consciousness of Divine Mother as an orb of energy that I lifted up to my heart before it dissipated into the ethers of the land around us.

imani began to sing and play her Hang once again. She called in my ancestors and my medicine to mark this initiation. I made offerings of water to earth, sky, and Venus in gratitude for the incredible experience. When it was complete, imani brought a blue blanket out of her basket and offered it to me with prayer and blessings, placing it around my shoulders.

This was the state of silent ecstasy I was in when I heard my primary guide, Grandmother Bone Womyn, task me with a vision. I was wrapped in this light-blue fuzzy blanket beneath the stars, by the fire. The group was dispersing and exchanging small talk. I had no words to express what had just happened, as it made no sense to my rational brain, so I remained in a space of deep inner listening. That was when I heard Bone Womyn speaking to me.

> "My daughter," she said, "You must gather the bones. This is the next step, the one you have been waiting for. Gather the bones of Sheila and the bones of Peter and place them together within you.
>
> "You must understand who he is, who his people are... Find his relatives... You need to walk on their land, touch their soil, hear their stories.
>
> "You must call to you all that you know of your mother, the essence that inspired her spirit, and become conscious of how both of these elements join together in you.
>
> "It is time for the seed of compassion to unfurl."

Journal questions: Collective healing

- Do you feel called to examine your own trauma in light of collective healing?
- If you don't, is that okay with you? If it isn't, what is needed in order to come to peace with your choice?
- If you do, what societal issues are present in your story?
- What do you need to know about these issues?
- What is needed for you to begin to walk in the shoes of the other?

Ceremony: Planting the seed of collective vision

Season: The stone you have been working with throughout this book will need to sit in the ground for six months, so if you live where the ground freezes over half of the year, begin when the soil can be worked in the spring. If you live where the soil can be worked year-round, choose a six-month segment that aligns with planting times for your area.

Tools: offerings (personally prepared or those listed in Appendix), your stone, a small spade/shovel/spoon for digging, a seed, such as apple, pear, or any other fruit growing in your area, a small piece of the same fruit, flowers, journal, pen.

Location: must be outside. Find the most magnificent tree in your area, one that most definitely represents the tree of life. Go there at least once before you begin this ceremony, to ask permission to work there. Leave whatever offerings it asks for.

Intention: To align your personal vision of healing with its collective counterpart. Take time to journal and get clear on what your personal vision of healing is. Use the answers you have formulated from previous journal questions.

Trauma as Medicine

Notice the connection between your trauma, healing, and societal issues on a grander scale.

Proceed outside to the tree.

> Create sacred space, pray out loud, sing, rattle, or drum, and state your intention.
>
> - Connect with your energy body for ten minutes, opening it to this powerful tree of life, and notice what it feels like to connect. Journal as needed.
>
> - Repeat your intention again: that you would like to align your personal vision of healing with a collective vision of healing.
>
> - Ask the spirit of this tree where you may plant this vision at its base.
>
> - Dig a small hole, maybe a foot deep.
>
> - Place offerings in the hole. These could be to your ancestors, to the Grandmothers and Grandfathers of the land you are on, to Spirit, or to the great Mother, to guide you and support you. Be creative and follow your intuition.
>
> - Next, blow your intention into your stone with three strong exhales. This stone is a powerful healing ally, having been with you through all of the processes in this book, and now you are aligning it with the collective healing vision of our planet, unique to your trauma. Feel gratitude for it, and place it in the earth with love.
>
> - Now, pick up the seed; this stands for potentiality. Ask for Spirit to align you wholeheartedly in carrying the wisdom inherent in this seed within yourself to grow this vision. Blow this into the seed and place it in the earth.
>
> - Pick up the flower; this represents opening to the beauty of the universe. Ask Spirit to align you with taking the time needed to flower this vision, to appreciate its beauty, and to reach for the highest light. Blow this into the flower and place it in the earth.
>
> - Pick up the fruit; this represents manifestation of the full cycle. Ask Spirit to align you with the fullest capacity of your being on a collective level,

> and to make room for savouring the fruit of your endeavours. Blow this into the fruit and place it in the earth.
> - Say any remaining prayers that feel right for you.
> - Cover the hole.
>
> Close the sacred space with gratitude.

Your ceremony does not end there. Visit the tree at the full moon and the new moon to pray and leave offerings. Connect your energy body to the tree and listen, sense, and feel its guidance. Inquire in your journal as to how your personal healing work is aligning with being of service on a collective level.

After six months, create your own ceremony to dig up the stone. It is now charged and aligned with the collective vision you are seeking. Sit with this over the winter months or the following six months. How does your stone feel different now? What is this collective vision? How is it guiding you to take action? What must you change within yourself to follow through? What must you open to?

Spirit will guide you

For those of you who feel the drive to collective healing, Spirit will plant seeds that open a path that is unique to you. Your map will be different from mine, but it will hold similar markers, such as the ability to be compassionate, curious, and willing to lay down personal hurt for the sake of vaster understanding.

You will be triggered. Remember that a trigger is simply energy that needs tending. You will be afraid, and the fear will not go away. However, as you walk with it, you will begin to recognize it as another teacher on the path. You will want to stop—more than once—and you may, until that drive ignites again, compelling you forward. Hold your helping spirits near to your heart, practice the exercises in this book, and place your prayers in the hands of the Spirit to guide your way.

CHAPTER 11:
The Colonial Wound

> "White-body supremacy trauma is a trauma that we all—including white-identified individuals, communities and systems—integrate into our bodies and structures. We need to address this trauma directly in our bodies, not just in our minds."
>
> Resmaa Manakem, *My Grandmother's Hands*

Saddle Lake Cree Nation lies three hours northwest of Edmonton, in Treaty 6 territory. This was the traditional land of Peter's people, and this was where I knew I needed to go to follow the vision I had been tasked with.

In November of 2010, I was on my way there. I had contacted the band shortly after the bone-gathering vision, sharing a little bit of my story, and their Chief and Council, through the Tribal Administrator, had appointed former chief Eric Large to work with me.

The next few years gave me a profound education in the history of colonization in Canada and in the rich cultural traditions of the Saddle Lake Cree. Much of what I learned came from working with Eric, the stories he shared with me, and the cultural events or ceremonies I was included in. I was invited on several occasions to come and share my story through the Resolution Health support services for the Saddle Lake area where Eric worked. This included workshops at Saddle Lake and working in the tipi at the Blue Quills Culture camp. In time, it evolved through word of mouth to workshops and conferences around Alberta.

In the workshops, I told my story and invited others to share in a talking circle. The ones that stand out the most in my mind are from Blue Quill, when elders joined us in the tipi, drinking muskeg tea around the fire. One elder in particular shared stories of growing up on the reserve. He remembered not being allowed to leave or sell anything without permission from the Indian agent, and the struggles his father had trying to feed his family. He held a braid of sweetgrass as he spoke, and paused to touch it every now and then, as if it was helping him gather his words.

As my work developed into trauma-focused healing workshops and private healing sessions with many First Nations clients, I could not believe the epidemic level of trauma. For many, it went beyond personal issues into an essence that felt deeper. It felt collective. It was binding, toxic, and hard to heal... hard to name. The trauma was elusive and difficult to pinpoint, with so many contributing factors it was almost undefinable. I knew it didn't belong solely to the individual I was supporting or the groups I was working with. It felt too ancestral, too big. I started to recognize it as the colonial wound. It was one of the main links to my own story that I was called to bring attention to.

The Impact of Colonization

The following comes from what I have gathered from my own experiences, people's stories, and my own reading. It in no way does justice to the full weight of colonial destruction, and it is still expressed through the lens of my own white privilege. Be that as it may, it is what I have, and it is part of what fulfilling my Bone Gathering task led me to learn.

Since the beginning of the colonial empire, the constructs of society and its institutions have been developed to benefit the colonizers. The Church and European governments dictated Christian dominion and superiority over all lands inhabited by non-Christians, justifying their ability to seize and colonize any lands they "discovered." Because First Nations were considered to be savages in need of assimilation and salvation, the fact that they had been on the land first did not hold credibility over the power and supremacy of the White colonizers.

When Treaties were signed (including Treaty Six in 1876), Indigenous people were fed the illusion that they would keep their sovereignty and right of self-determination as First Nations peoples. There was a sense they would be able to maintain their culture and ways of life. This was not the case; in fact, everything within the power of the government was done to ensure this was not so.

The buffalo were the source of everything for many Indigenous people: providing food, hides for shelter, bones for tools, and more. Those herds were intentionally massacred—slaughtered by the millions for their tongues and hides—the rest left to rot. With the elimination of their food source, the people became dependent on handouts from the Indian agents, as the land they were allotted in treaty signing was not prime farmland. Plus, they had no knowledge of farming; it was a whole new way of living to learn. Though many did in time, the government was quick to set up restrictions to ensure they were not successful. The pass system was enforced from 1885 to 1951, which meant they were not allowed to leave the reserve without permission or sell goods without written consent from the Indian agent (who was, needless to say, not First Nations). For a First Nations person with treaty status, it was impossible to be self-sufficient or sustainable in what was rapidly becoming a western world.

This is our Canadian history, which has been brought to the surface on a more public scale only recently. For years, history was told solely by white males, which meant almost anything to do with First Nations was depicted in a derogatory format and seen as *less than* the white man. To this day, the energy thread of white supremacy is clear in the dominion of the Indian Act. It was set up in 1876 with the sole intention to control native status, land, resources, wills, education, and band administration. Though it has been amended through the years, it is still in effect today.

From 1885 to 1951, the Indian Act banned many First Nations ceremonies—the Potlatch, Sun Dance, and Sweat Lodge, to name a few. They were labeled as evil and against God. First Nations' ways of praying, purifying, and communicating with what was holy and sacred to them became something that had to be hidden.

Residential schools were set up and enforced as mandatory by 1920. In the treaties, education had been a part of the agreement, though First Nations likely assumed teachers would come to the reserves to teach. That did not suit the intention of the government, which was to eradicate cultures and traditions, so boarding schools became the law. Parents were arrested if they did not give up their children. The RCMP went to take all school-age children from their homes. Some Native people moved further into the bush to hide, but then they were isolated from their community.

At the schools, the children's clothes were taken away and they were given a school uniform; their hair was shaved, and they were deloused. They were not allowed to be with siblings of the opposite sex, who were housed in different dorms. They were punished for speaking their own language, for any behaviour that was not considered proper, or simply because First Nations kids were not considered to be human and thus were not treated as such. Sexual abuse, physical abuse, starvation, and isolation were used as punishment. Kids were pitted against each other and did not feel safe anywhere. The formal intention was to "Kill the Indian in the child" (a literal statement accredited to Prime Minster John A. Macdonald in the late 1800s and acknowledged in a formal apology by Prime Minister Steven Harper in 2008), believing they would become proper functioning Christian adults who could be a part of civilized society and leave the Indian way behind them. Parents were only able to see their children in the summer—in some cases, not for years. Many kids died when they tried to run away and ended up freezing to death in their attempt to make it home.

Of course the residential school system didn't work. The children didn't fit into the overculture when they left the schools. The unresolved childhood trauma and abuse from the schools caused addiction, violence, and more cycles of abuse. Most were distanced from their culture and had no healthy outlet to recover. There was no access to resources or support.

The "Sixties Scoop" brought the next wave of trauma. By now, whole generations had grown up in residential schools like their parents before them. Without any experience of having been parented, they were raising children in underserved communities rampant with poverty, high death rates, and socio-economic barriers.

Throughout the 1960s, provincial child welfare agencies continued to seize children. Residential schools might be gone, but now families lost their children to foster care, where many were subjected to abuses and neglect similar to their parents before them.

The source of Peter's evil

When I met Eric, the first thing he shared with me was information about teen suicide among First Nations kids. The numbers were so mind-boggling to me that I couldn't understand why there wasn't attention being raised on a provincial or national level. All I could think was, "Why isn't anyone doing anything about this? How could this be happening *here*, a few hours from my home?!" I lived in a community right beside the First Nations reserve of Maskwacis, and I had not heard about this from any of my neighbours. I realized that much was hidden because of the dominant culture's impact and control of point of view, as well as shame.

The energy of this history is present in all Treaty people. It is present globally in all colonizers and those who are colonized. It will not be healed or resolved until the dominant culture takes responsibility for their part in it. The truth needs to be acknowledged, validated, and lived—in actions, not words, by ordinary people, not just government officials and organizations.

It is not in the past. It is still happening. The Indian Act remains the legislation that governs and controls First Nations in Canada to this day.

What is missing in any talks on reconciliation is what we of settler origin are responsible for. We have to make amends. Energetically, we are tied through our ancestors and history to the present-day trauma we so often close our eyes to.

It is easy for the dominant white culture to say, "This is not my issue. Why don't they get over it? I am so tired of the Indian problem." It's easy to avoid when you are not the one being marginalized, stereotyped, judged, and suppressed every day. It's easy to ignore when your own ancestors created the situation and you don't want to face that reality or take responsibility for it.

The truth is, there was a cost to our ancestor's homesteads. Whether they were ignorant of it or not, the land had a price higher than the sweat and tears they used to clear it and claim it. It was the blood, tears, and culture of those who had lived there for thousands of years.

I have referenced homicide as taking us into the bowels of the underworld with a visceral understanding of the evil that human beings are capable of. Here is the thread of connection. Here is the link to the source of Peter's evil. It is a consequence of colonialism and the genocide of First Nations people.

When someone's power is taken from them for generations, they will do what they can to get it back. For Peter Brighteyes, that meant violence.

Naming the trauma

To metabolize trauma, we need to name the source of the energy and go through the digestion process of assimilating its gifts and releasing its unhealthy bits. When trauma is intergenerational, compounded, and continuous, the act of naming is really difficult. An Indigenous participant in a Trauma and Transformation program I was teaching said to me recently, "How can you name what you were born into? How can you identify all of the pieces when they came from everywhere?" I had no answer for this, aside from the knowing that as humans, all we can do is take one step at a time from where we are now, with what is present in the moment. The rest is revealed at each step by listening to Spirit and asking for help.

Dancing home

In May of 2011, I participated in a traditional Chicken Dance at the Blue Quills culture camp. It was a bright, sunny day with the sweetness of poplar resin in the air, the prairie breeze fresh on my skin.

The ceremony was in a large outdoor structure that was about 80 feet long, 30 feet across, and 20 feet high, made mostly from the trees that grew on the land. The top opened to the sky. The upper branches tilted inwards to meet in the centre above us and somehow were tied together. There was a white tarp around the sides from ground level to about ten feet up. Inside were over one hundred and fifty people, women seated on the left, men on the right, some in chairs against the white tarp in the shade, others on the ground on blankets. I didn't notice this when I first went in, so I headed towards the right side and sat down on the ground cross-legged. Shortly thereafter, an auntie came over and gently instructed me on some of the traditional protocols, particularly which side to sit on.

In the centre, there was room for women to dance, and a few were waiting for the music to start again. Men danced near the drums. At the far end sat the elders, and before them, the drummers and singers. The main drum was large—probably three feet across—and it was held on a stand, with four or more men sitting around it. I had heard this type of drum before at powwows and at my children's elementary school. (Their school was half First Nations and shared bi-cultural teachings.) When played, it drew my focus inward to the primal sensation of the beat, where nothing mattered or existed beyond the present moment.

I could feel my mother's spirit with me as I stood with the ladies waiting to dance. My mind traced the trail of years and experiences that had brought me to this moment, and I felt such sadness—not only for the loss of my mother, but for the losses these people have had to face. I was there as a presenter, and in the past few days I had shared my story many times in the Resolution Support Services Tipi. But most importantly, I had been listening to the stories of others, and I was struck by the sheer magnitude of grief.

The drummers and singers started to play, and I felt Peter's spirit join me. Two hawks circled overhead as I began to move with the rhythm of the sound. Tears fell down my cheeks as my heart opened to all of this loss—this senseless loss. The dance became a prayer, a way to honour all that had transpired to bring me here, a tribute to my mother and her legacy of choosing love over hate. As I moved, I felt like Peter was not only dancing with me, but dancing through me. I cried for him and all he would never be. I wasn't sure if his feet had ever danced on this land, and I wondered what would've happened if his life had turned out differently—if he would be up there with the other men, drumming and dancing the traditional Chicken Dance. As I pondered this, I felt him dance away from me, through the crowd of women dancers, in and out of the circle of male dancers near the drum, past the elders, through the walls of this sacred structure, and out onto the land, beyond the realm of my vision.

"*He is dancing himself home,*" I thought to myself.

The singing stopped, and a sacred pipe was passed before the elders. I sat near a woman I had spoken with earlier in the week. She told me this dance was a way of honouring those who have crossed over. I smiled at her and told her that made perfect sense to me.

Sarah Salter-Kelly

Sacred tears

A few weeks later, I wrote a blog post about my experience, which found its way to the provincial liaison for the Truth and Reconciliation Commission of Canada, Darlene Auger. She emailed me, asking if she could record my story for the TRC archives. Initially, I was a little confused. Weren't those recordings of First Nations peoples' stories? However, she was attracted to my understanding of the collective impact of colonization, and felt this was important to document. We arranged for her to come to my house and record my story.

Interestingly enough, the day Darlene came to do this was February seventeenth, 2012, my mother's birthday. She would have been 59 years old.

We smudged with the sage she brought with her, and I was given a stone to hold while I spoke. It had been painted by school children with the intention of helping the story-gathering process. A basket was placed before me alongside a box of tissues. Darlene said a prayer in Cree and told me that my tears were sacred, so any tissues I used were to be put in the basket and honoured in a ceremonial way.

I was nervous and excited to share. She told me that once the recorder was turned on and I began to speak, she would not speak at all.

By this time, I had shared my story publicly on many occasions. But there was something different this time. It could have been the deep space of listening Darlene created, or that we were in the comfort of my healing centre on my land.

When I came to the part in my story of becoming aware of the suffering that my First Nations brothers and sisters have gone through, something broke inside of me and I started to cry. There were so many stories and tragedies spiralling through my mind, cracking me open.

"I am so sorry," I said. "I don't know at what level my ancestors were involved, but I am sorry for whatever ways they were."

CHAPTER 12:

Healing with Marilyn, Peter's Sister

> "Hope is kindled when we remember
> that we belong to one another.
>
> By dropping our impulse to otherise, reclaiming our kinship with all life, and embracing the Earth as our Mother, we can collectively awaken from this dangerous dream of dominance and take up the privilege of stewardship that all the great wisdom traditions remind us is our true task."
>
> –Mirabai Starr, *Wild Mercy*

I knew Peter had a sister named Marilyn. Back in 1996, she had been in a CBC documentary called *Beating the Streets*, and I found her through Facebook a few weeks after the bone-gathering vision. She was not living in Alberta at the time, so I could not meet with her when I first went to Saddle Lake. She was open to answering my questions through texts or a phone call, but it was hard to correspond about such intense content in those formats. We were finally able to meet in person for the first time in May of 2012.

It was during Culture Camp, on the grounds of Blue Quill College. This was the former residential school Marilyn's mother and sisters had gone to. I had toured the school the day before, so the reality of what her family had experienced was fresh in my mind. We spent the day walking the grounds—the grounds that had instigated such trauma in her family, and likely the roots of my mother's murder.

Marilyn is forthcoming, honest, and to the point. She was clear that, being thirteen years younger than Peter, she had not grown up with him, and she had only experienced violence from him. She could not tell his story to me, but she could tell hers, and endeavor to answer whatever questions I might have through the lens of her experience.

What happened that day, and has continued through the years, is a soul sharing of profound loss, coupled with one of the most amazing stories I have ever heard of resilience and recovery.

I was initially surprised by how much I liked Marilyn, and how comfortable it was to speak with her.

Having grown up in violence and addiction, she painted a sordid picture of suffering that transfixed me with every syllable. She does not hold back when she shares; she speaks with the courage to dispel the shame that arises when trauma is repressed or denied. Her story touched my heart then, and it continues to do so every time I hear it. After our first meeting, we eventually began to do public talks together, sharing our stories as voices for reconciliation and change.

Marilyn's stories didn't show me much of Peter's humanity. If anything, his violence was amplified. But through our conversations about trauma, compassion, and transformation, *she* started to consider the humanity within him for the first time—and noticed he never did have much of a chance.

What I came to love and respect about Marilyn right away was her ability to ask difficult questions and have hard conversations that many people avoid due to societal taboos. One of the questions she boldly asked me that first time we met was, "Why was your mother so important? Native women are murdered all the time, and nobody cares. I'm not trying to be rude, but what's the difference here?" Her question had no threat or challenge in it. Instead, it was an opportunity to discuss disparity and look at the truth. All the resources the city had were used to find my mother when she went missing. Volunteers came from far and wide to help search. Over 20 years later, people still remember her name.

Between 1980 and 2012, over 1200 murdered and missing Indigenous women were reported in Canada; likely the numbers are far greater. When an

Indigenous woman goes missing, it is often weeks before anything is done, and the level of investment by police and community is drastically different than what I experienced with my mom. The difference created through racial stereotypes and discrimination costs lives.

I didn't have an answer for her, other than that I was happy that my mother was important and that her body was found. However, I also was not ignorant to the disparity and injustice.

Marilyn and I talked about another crime Peter had committed—the torture of a guard in prison—and what may have motivated him. She stated, "I am not excusing him at all. He was a violent man, but you have to understand what it's like to be a Native man in prison. You have to understand how you are treated like scum. You are nothing, the lowest of the low. Eventually, there is going to be a consequence to that treatment."

The first evening we met, I went to her house. In an unusual series of events, Peter's AA book had come into my hands, and I wanted to give it to her. In the back was a note from a friend of his, commending him on the positive changes he had made and thanking him for helping her find herself. This note is dated almost a year before he killed my mother, and it finishes with "Most of all, keep on loving yourself." I added that information to the bundle of bones I was gathering—that he was a man who not only helped his friend find herself, but who was capable of conversations about self-love. He had the awareness to consider who he was and what he wanted as a human being in his life, at least in that moment.

Inside Marilyn's house, she told me about experiences from a recent life-skills coaching program she had completed. I marvelled over the synchronicity between my mother also being a life coach and what appeared to be a shared philosophy. What were the chances of that?

She pulled out some family albums to look at over tea, which constituted a moment in which I almost lost it entirely. It happened when she flipped the page and Peter's face appeared before me. It was all I could do to breathe. My body froze. I had only ever seen him at the trial, and in one picture that was used repeatedly in the newspapers and the trial. Seeing him in different clothes, situations, and facial expressions caught me off guard.

None of the healing work I had done, or the fact that I spoke to him regularly in spirit, mattered in that moment. For at least three breaths, I was in shock, paralyzed, wondering what the hell I was doing here. I kept breathing, it passed, and the focus of the bone gathering vision reminded me why I had come. I needed to do this, to face this, to understand the influences and experiences that had made Peter a murderer. What I was facing mattered.

So I looked at the pictures, every single one of them, listening to Marilyn's stories and family anecdotes with each turn of the page.

Shared healing

Three years passed before Marilyn and I first shared our stories in a public healing circle at Blue Quills College (it was the Resolution Health support services that brought us in, using Blue Quill's space). It was May of 2015, and many synchronistic events had transpired to bring this together. A few weeks prior, while in Peru on my way to the Amazon, I'd had a dream that I was to get this talk professionally filmed, and somehow, despite the distance and short amount of time, it came together.

I knew from experience that the content would need healers other than myself and Marilyn to hold the space, and I asked the college if traditional cultural support was possible. They connected us to Leo and Priscilla Mcgilvery, whom I met the night before at a ceremony they both led. It felt really good that they would be with us in the room. The rest of the group was people from all around Alberta who came to the Culture Camp for training and healing.

Leo suggested that Marilyn and I each hold a stone while we spoke from the centre altar, where I had created a circle mandala of rocks around the word *forgiveness*.

That was a hard circle to lead. I couldn't lead it, in fact, and I knew this. I felt very conscious of Marilyn's feelings, and interestingly enough, I felt a desire to protect her from the graphic details of Mom's homicide. I had never shared my experience in full with her. Normally when I did a public share, I jumped right into what happened, but this time, with her beside me, I found myself looking for softer ways to say it, conscious I was talking about her brother.

Then when Marilyn shared, she surprised me (and likely everyone in the room) by apologizing to *me* near the end of her share. At that moment, everything inside of me changed. Through her words and her presence, I was seen. My grief was seen. It was unexpected, raw, and real. I felt transformed.

The following is a direct transcription of her words:

> I can honestly say, my brother Peter, you know, he had hurt me, but everyone in my family had hurt me, you know. But that's how they grew up; that's what they knew. And when they chose not to go into that, they just continued the cycle. And when I was listening to you talk about your... your mom, you know, I was sitting here thinking, *"What did you do, Peter?"* You know. **I'm sorry that he hurt you and your family**. I knew what he was capable of. But I also know that he was a little boy. You know, I remember through the training we're always taught that—we're always told that we're born perfect, whole, and complete—it's through family, friends, society, that we learn how to become hurtful. And I know also I can't change the past. I have no control over it.
>
> And the way I show my sorrow or—how do you say that? To make amends. The way I learned to make amends is by changing the cycle, and that's what I'm doing with my children. Everything that I learn I teach them, like your mother (did). I do that with my children now. Because I learned that it starts, starts here, you know. And I remember, like, I'm hiking all the time and caught a ride with one elder and he said, "Do you know the seven directions? Seven directions, you know. He goes, well, north, east, west, south, Mother Earth, Father Sky, and the most important one within." And that's where it's always got to start. And that's what I've done. And that's what I teach my children.
>
> I can't, I can't help my family; I've tried. And I can't help anyone. All I can do is share my story and the struggles that I have and continue to have, you know. I struggle with depression and I struggle with so much that comes along with FASD [Fetal Alcohol Spectrum Disorder]. And I realize that a lot of my beginnings were the secondary effects of FASD and that's what my family, my brothers and sisters, have lived. And I understand that now. And now I can live with this. But I'm really grateful. I'm thankful that you invited me to share. It's—I haven't had the easiest life, but you know, we all have our struggles. And when we each are blessed with angels, and I call them angels, those who come and change your life and change your way of thinking and just save you. And they're always there in our lives and it's always

> our choice on whether or not we want to utilize them. You know. Because so many times it's so easy to say, well, I know they're trying to help and I just don't want to be a burden. But that's letting ego and not Spirit control you. And it's tough because you get them mixed up. So thank you very much for having me here.

When Marilyn finished speaking, there was a palpable shift in the energy of the room—an opening in the ethers of what reconciliation can be.

Leo Mcgilvery asked Marilyn and me if he could a sing a song for us because Marilyn had apologized to me and he wanted to honour that. Could we hold hands as well and face each other? Their song in Cree wrapped a blanket around us, marked by Leo's drum and Priscilla's rattle. We held hands, with each other's stones still in them, and when the song was done, we traded stones. I wanted the chance to walk with this woman's story.

I could feel our ancestors with us, and I wondered what Mom and Marilyn's mother, Olivine, thought of each other. Did they have any influence on this event, happening here on this land?

Journal questions: Considering the bigger picture

- ▶ What difficult conversations do you need to have, and with whom, to address conflict related to your trauma and collective vision?
- ▶ What steps can you take to initiate these conversations? List them here.
- ▶ How can you use what you learn to have a real-life impact on the world around you?
- ▶ For those of settler origin, are there actions you can take to make amends or reparation of harm towards the colonial wound? What does this look like for you?

CHAPTER 13:
The Sacred Hoop

"We may not be responsible for the world that
created our minds, but we can take responsibility
for the mind with which we create our world."

—*Gabor Maté, In the Realm of the Hungry Ghosts, Close Encounters with Addiction*

"To touch the earth is an act of
reconciliation, not an act of worship.

It is an act of coming home to what is here and what is now.

It is an act of embracing and being
embraced by our mother Earth."

—*Thich Nhat Hanh, Together We Are One*

> May 2016
>
> I offer tobacco at each of the four directions, touching the Sacred Hoop of a Hundred Eagle feathers as I do so... eyes closed in prayer... my question the same at each direction as I contemplate this book, my work here on this planet, and what it all means.

> "Great Spirit, show me how to be of service... How do I take this story and offer it up as a means to make a difference? Guide me in creating a bridge between nations... guide me in giving voice to reconciliation... teach me how to listen... show me what I need to do... I am at your service."

My heart is scratched open and raw. I am humbled by the stories I have heard, not only at this event, but in the many circles I have been in within First Nations communities.

These stories elicit compassion and sometimes shock at the level of compound trauma and suffering. They have taught me of my white privilege. There was a time I would have said *I don't notice race*, not realizing that was because I was never treated differently. I have not once experienced the stereotypes, judgments, and discrimination that is definitely part of the daily life of someone who is not white.

My body shifts in sync with the ceremony, its rhythm moving through my blood into every cell. There are four grandmothers, or *kokums*, as is said in Cree, singing traditional songs and rattling in front of the group as each person takes their turn to offer their prayers in the form of tobacco at the Hoop.

I smell sweetgrass and sage, prairie flowers and rain. I feel the energy from the ceremony amplified through the quantity of people and the earnestness of prayer. Though most prayers are spoken softly, something changes within each of us as we participate. It is a ceremony of commitment and holds the intensity of such.

The Hoop is made of the four colours of all Nations: black, red, white, and yellow. It is about two feet in diameter, resting horizontally to the earth on a stand about four feet high. All around, one hundred eagle feathers are tied, hanging from ribbons blowing in the wind, with one in the centre to represent the missing and murdered Indigenous women of Canada. That one was added especially for this event.

The Hoop was born of a vision that came to Don Coyhis, an American of the Mohican Nation, who is the Keeper of the Hoop and a member of the White Bison Society. He came to this event in collaboration with a local non-profit organization, the Kis Sai Wah Toe Tat Towin Win society. White Bison offers an approach to healing for addiction called the Wellbriety Movement. It combines Indigenous teachings, ceremony, and spiritual practices in a form that is sustainable, as it focuses on personal ownership, healing of trauma, and connection to community. In fact, the main intention is creating sober communities, which is why KSWTITS brought the White Bison Society to this event. The death toll from suicide, addiction, and the consequences of historical trauma in this area's reserves have been astronomical, like so many communities across Canada, instigating the coming of the Sacred Hoop and the creation of this ceremonial event.

We are upriver from the city of Rocky Mountain House, standing on the land where the first European settlers—fur traders and explorers, mostly—met the Ancestors of this land, the Cree and the Nakoda. There is a historic site over the hill to the north that depicts what it was like to be on this land beside the North Saskatchewan River one hundred and twenty-five years ago. That was when the fur trade was pushing its way as far west as possible, seeking passage through the Rocky Mountains. Of course, this historic site is primarily constructed from the perspective of the white settlers, with homage to the birth of Canada. I am sure it is not necessarily viewed in the same way by the First Nations.

In many ways, the consequences of that first meeting instigated the need for this healing camp. Gathered here are people who have been directly or indirectly affected by residential schools and colonization, be that broken treaties, exploitation, or cultural degradation. Most are First Nations People seeking a means to sustainably heal their wounds. Others come to create a bridge between nations. Each person has a story to share, and the custom of Indigenous teachings recognizes that each story and their sharing brings healing to the whole.

It is in this belief in story-sharing that I have been asked to attend. Tomorrow, Marilyn and I will hold a circle in the large tipi. The floor is laid with buffalo robes, and there is plenty of room for a large group. This is the fifth time in one year that Marilyn and I have shared our stories together. I feel an unexpected love for this woman. Every time we are together, it changes who I am. It is difficult and uncomfortable. It is inspiring and moving.

My commitment is to do justice to this experience that has so deeply impacted my life—to share my belief that reconciliation in Canada demands more than token acts. It asks something of each of us, particularly those of the majority—white folks—that we have the courage to listen to and consider a point of view and perspective other than our own. And through this act of listening—deep, soul-felt listening—we may come to a solution or outcome that honours the integrity and the power of all involved.

We are not separate from each other. One person or one nation's suffering becomes poison when ignored, rejected, and discredited; poison that spreads like wildfire and scorches us all. Mom's death was the result of this fire. Once burning, it's a fire that is unpredictable and sometimes unstoppable.

Our commitment as a nation must be to do whatever it takes to stop ignoring these fires. Stop pretending they do not exist, they are not important, or they belong on the reserve with the "Indians," as it is "their" problem, not ours.

For me today, this commitment is about honouring Mom's legacy by being willing to walk the path of freedom and forgiveness, no matter how difficult or scary that might be for me. I consider how unusual it was for Dad to have had traditional moccasins made for Mom when she died—and who, at the guidance of my cousin, who is First Nations, also placed tobacco and sweetgrass in her coffin for the ancestors of this land. When I recently asked him why, he had completely forgotten about it. He had simply been following his gut.

I hold my commitment in my heart at each direction as I touch the Sacred Hoop. It is said to bring forth healing. It is said to answer prayers.

Touching the Hoop at the final direction, I am hit by a sense of knowing: not the kind with a direct answer, which I had hoped for, but the kind that instantaneously tells me I must do all I can to bring this story forward. That I will know what to do.

Stepping away from the Hoop, I am brushed from front to back with an eagle wing and smudged with cedar. It brushes the dust from my scars, removes the shield on my heart, and beckons me to use my voice. To speak. To simply tell the story.

To *trust*.

Epilogue

By the time this book is published, it will be 25 years since my mother was murdered. I have felt her with me all along, encouraging me (sometimes forcefully) to get the book done.

This has been very difficult to write. The personal nature of the task at hand and the picking apart of my process to find the medicine in a way that is comprehensible and useful for you, the reader, had to be done slowly and thoroughly. Regardless of this, I am sure there are things I have forgotten or elements that may be confusing. I have, after all, transferred vision, heart, and spirit into the analytical format of paper and pen (okay, laptop and keyboard), and no matter how carefully I did it, some of the essence is bound to be lost along the way.

This process of writing and formulating, cutting and scripting has been over seven years in the making. For much of that time, I struggled with being seen in my whole story. At times I was more focused on who my audience would be and how I would meet their needs over the innate call to speak my truth. Was it a book for shamanic students, energy healers, or for someone looking to heal trauma? It has been my experience that the two are not always one and the same. Was it for those connected to reconciliation in Canada, or, for that matter, restorative justice, as I have spoken at events for both? How does this all fit together, I wondered. In moments of insecurity, my head masterminded my heart, and an internal war was waged over the right way to use my voice.

In the fall of 2018, when I became older than my mother would ever be, there was a palpable shift in my life. It culminated in a midlife pause, and by the summer of 2019, my husband and I, together with our last child at home, sold everything we owned—our five-bedroom farmhouse, seven acres, my healing centre barn, and most of our possessions—for a simpler life one thousand kilometres away, in the southern mountains of B.C. In some ways, I was at the tail end of being a "hands-on" mother in that my twins had left home. I could consciously move into and consider the next part of my life. Here I was, living days, weeks, and months beyond my mother, and I needed to make use of this gift of time. To honour the life I had that my mother did not. The time had come to choose my heart and trust that somehow, all of the components in this story would fit together, and that they would make their way to the right people. The time had come to give voice to what my mom could not.

It is my hope that you, the reader, have found a nugget of inspiration in these pages and that there has been something in my story, or the exercises and teachings, that sparks your ability to believe in yourself and find what you need to move into the confining space of your own trauma.

The medicine I derived from this experience has blasted open my heart with compassion and the awareness that we humans are all in this together. For you who are new to this philosophy or at the beginning stages of your journey, I implore you to trust yourself and treat yourself with love and kindness, knowing that you will work through what is needed in the moment. Use the exercises in this book to discover the cords of energy that are the most important to address at this time, and the rest will be revealed to you along the path.

By listening to Spirit, you will be led in a sacred way. That is how it works. As time unfolds, there will be moments when you want to stop and turn back the clock to comfortable ignorance, or the contraction of holding all of the pain in. Healing is hard work, no matter what you visualize. It is *supposed* to be uncomfortable. When the caterpillar enters the cocoon, she literally has to turn to mush before she can transform into a butterfly. You, too, will turn to mush and shapeshift in this process.

As I join these final pieces together, the world is a few months into the COVID-19 pandemic and the rising of the Black Lives Matter movement. It is the summer of 2020. Our world needs us to be present, conscious, and willing to do the work to heal trauma. We each have a role to play in our personal and collective transformation. What we do with our lives matters.

I pray that you may hear the call to heal rise up within you, and that its song may align you with your reason for coming to this planet. What we need to heal is already here.

With love,
Sarah Salter Kelly
White Raven Woman
Summer Solstice 2020

APPENDIX:

—

Tools for Ceremony

Invocation of sacred space

Sacred space is created to generate a safe container for healing and ceremony. There are many ways to do this; consider the "Tree of Life" prayer I shared in the beginning of this book in contrast to the ones I share below. They are each unique and effective. What is important is that you feel like you have named, claimed, and marked what is holy and sacred to you, to be present. In this way Spirit directs the course of the ceremony rather than your own mind/ego.

The energy of prayer is a conductive force used throughout our world to open the heart to Spirit. Allow yourself to be curious as to its mechanics on a personal level. In other words, inquire for yourself internally as to what words you can use to generate a space that feels safe and healing for you. Alternately, use the ones I have included, perhaps as cues to contemplate what you would say if you were to write your own.

Sacred Space - Simple Opening

I open myself to the Great Mystery
Cast your light upon me, within me, and around me
Illuminate this space and mark it as Holy and Sacred

I breathe you in from the four quarters...
The north, the east, the south and the west...
I breathe you in from the earth below, and from the heavens above

Help me to be present in my body
To still the busyness of my mind,
Help me open my heart to this moment, to what is here now

May it be so.

Sarah Salter-Kelly

Sacred Space: The Seven Directions

To open, face each of the directions in sequence, moving clockwise. (When you close the circle later, move counter-clockwise, changing your language so that you are thanking and releasing rather than calling in.)

Each direction corresponds to a season, an element, a time in the wheel of the year, and a body aspect, all of which I have included. These teachings first came to me through the Reclaiming Tradition, when I was in my teens, primarily influenced by Starhawk's book, *The Spiral Dance*. In almost thirty years of practice, I have found them to be invaluable. They are practical and comprehensive.

Most traditions have their own system that is unique to the dynamic energy therein, and many of these will contradict the other. There isn't a right or a wrong way to create sacred space or to place the elements within the directions, this is simply a map. And inasmuch its intention is to bring you to a destination – or an experience if you will - where your body, mind and spirit align to be present with your healing work. Let yourself explore what works best for you.

The teachings around the archetypes I am invoking, in particular the Eagle, the Mountain Lion, the Serpent and the Apus (sacred mountains), came into my practice through the influence Andean Shamanism. Note that south of the equator, the counterpart to the Eagle is the Condor, and to the Mountain Lion, the Jaguar.

East
  Spring
  Air
  Feb 2 – May 1
  Mental body

> To the winds of the east, place of the rising sun, I welcome you into this space.
>
> I call forth the elemental spirit of Air to be with me.
>
> Show me how to use my voice with power by aligning the crystal clarity of my mind with the deep knowing of my belly and drawing them together

in my heart. Let my words come from my heart centre on this day and all others.

I welcome in the Eagle, the master visionary, you who fly wing to wing with Great Spirit. May I climb upon your back and open myself to your vision. Help me see the greater picture. Liberate me from the bondage of my past and present by helping me see what steps I must take to move forward.

Wrap your wings of light around me and be with me in this ceremony.

I call forth the innocence of my child self. May she walk through the path set by the rising sun and guide me with her curiosity and wonderment. May her perspective of possibility lead me.

Blessed be.

South
    Summer
    Fire
    May 1 – August 2
    Spiritual body

To the winds of the south, I welcome you into this space.

I call forth the elemental spirit of Fire to be with me.

May I allow my spiritual nature to guide me and trust in the alchemical process of transformation. May I feel this force of fire within me.

I welcome in the Serpent, regenerator of life, you who move on the belly of the Mother. Help me feel her heartbeat in every cell of my body. Guide me to connect with my primal instincts, my passion, and my creativity, so this is the energy that motivates me. Help me shed the stories of limitation the way you shed your skin in one piece, without drama or attachment.

Wrap your coils of light around me and be with me in this ceremony.

I call forth the strength, tenacity, and action of my adult self. Help me to bring focus, decisiveness, and organization into my life. Help me to trust in the knowing that leads me at all times.

Blessed be.

West
    Fall
    Water
    Aug 2 – Oct 31
    Emotional body

To the winds of the west, place of the setting sun, I welcome you into this space.

I call forth the elemental spirit of Water to be with me.

May I trust in the flow of emotions that run through me, allowing grief, loss, and surrender to open me to a new way of knowing myself. May I be cleansed in the waters of this land and make time to listen to their song.

I welcome in the Mountain Lion, you who walk with power and precision. Teach me to find the courage to navigate the darkness of my own life's journey. Support me in facing fear and living wholeheartedly. Help me to release any sensation of powerlessness in my life.

I welcome in my elder self, you who are in the waning years of this journey, who can sit beside death and bring understanding to life. Guide me with your wisdom.

Blessed be.

North
    Winter
    Earth
    October 31 – February 2
    Physical body

To the winds of the north, I welcome you into this space.

I call forth the elemental spirit of Earth to be with me.

May I be present and centred in my physical body. May I generate a solid foundation from the inside out.

I welcome in the Ancestors.

Those of this land, I ask permission to work in ceremony here now. Those of my bloodline, I call you to guide me in transforming stories of generational bondage and to bring forth your gifts and talents in such away that I can dream a good dream for our future generations. Those of my soul path, help me connect with my tribe and satisfy my purpose for coming here. Help me be of service.

I welcome in the Sacred Mountains. (Say the names of all of the Sacred Mountains that you have a relationship with.) May this space be encircled with your infinite insight and wisdom.

I welcome in my Spirit self, the part of me in between the life/death/rebirth process. Support me in connecting to the chaos of the void.

Blessed be.

Mother Earth

Great Mother, Gaia, Pachamama, Blessed Mother, Mother-Maiden-Crone, by all the names by which you are known, I welcome you into this space.

Help me sink my roots deeply into you to find the spaces and places that nourish my body, mind, and spirit. Help me to slow down, stop, and listen to what is important. Help me to trust in turning inwards.

I give thanks to all my relations: the four-legged, two-legged, furred, feathered, and finned, those who swim in the deeps and those who fly in the air, the creepy crawlies, the plant people, the tree people, and all the food that feeds my body, mind, and spirit. I offer deep gratitude for all the nourishment I receive. May I use this awareness of abundance to transcend scarcity consciousness and come home to the realization that there is *enough*.

Teach me how to give back to you.

May this ceremony bring healing to all of our relations.

Blessed be.

Great Spirit

Great Spirit, Great Mystery, creator, Father, Son, and Holy Spirit, you who are known by a thousand names and you who are the nameless one, I welcome you into this space. I call forth the energy of protection and grace. I welcome in your love and your blessing.

Help me to be humble and bring humor to my adventures on this planet. Remind me to soften and open to what you have to share.

Illuminate the truth of who I am and allow that illumination to be the fuel that motivates me and inspires how I show up each day.

Help me to see the "other" as my brother or sister and come home to our shared humanity. Teach me to release the convictions of righteousness and judgment, be that towards myself or others.

I welcome in Grandmother Moon, Grandfather Sun, and the Starlight Nations.

Be with us.

Blessed be.

Self

I welcome in my helping spirits and guides. Help me to see what I need to see, hear what I need to hear, and embody what is important for this ceremony to unfold

I, [say your name], am present, open, and ready for the ceremony to begin.

Blessed be.

Offerings

Offerings are created and given—most often placed out on the land—to generate reciprocity and to give thanks. Sometimes, these thanks are part of a specific intention or ceremony, and other times they are simply to honour and give back for the abundance of our lives. They are a tangible way to acknowledge and live in balance with all of your relations.

There are no right or wrong offerings. I have been instructed by human teachers through the years that a piece of my hair, some of my saliva, or even my urine are practical offerings when given with prayer and intention. You can also send loving energy into the earth through your energy body, hand chakras, heart, etc. As a Reiki Master teacher, I use Reiki by first filling my whole being with its energy, and then transferring this divine light with intention into the earth.

When in doubt, ask. Be it the land, Spirit, or your guides, they will tell you. I have had Raven tell me to leave shiny doo-dads out in the trees, or meat for Wolf. Mandalas of flowers have been given to the Mother Earth or the spirit of the land I am living on. The ancestors have asked me for their favourite meals, crystals, tools, stones, and, most commonly, cornmeal and tobacco. The possibilities are endless.

Corn

This is an offering for the Grandmothers from what they have shared with me in North and South America. I am not familiar with those of other continents, and I suggest that you inquire for yourself with respect to the land that you are living on. Despite the fact that corn wasn't grown traditionally in the area of Canada in which I reside, it is still asked for by these Grandmothers. The offering may be in the form of cornmeal, kernels, or corn flour. In a pinch, I have even used popcorn. If you can grow your own corn, that is a beautiful process of caring for your relationship with the Grandmothers with intention.

When you are offering corn, call in the Grandmothers who work with you to be present (check out ancestral breakdown in Chapter 3) and say a prayer out loud to them before you place it on the land. I like to blow my prayers and thanks into the actual corn itself and then offer it.

Corn may also be used in reciprocity for plants, stones, or objects you are gathering from the land. Speak directly to the spirit of what you are gathering and lay the corn down with thanks.

Tobacco

This is an offering for the Grandfathers of this land—again, in North and South America; inquire for your own locale—though I have a feeling tobacco will still be the one.

Tobacco has many uses in earth-based traditions, ceremonies and healing practices. In this context, you are thanking those Grandfathers who work with you, as well as those who are connected to the land you are on.

As with all offerings, get the best of the best, as this demonstrates the value you place on what you are praying or giving thanks for. At the same time, use what you have. You want to put the effort in to offer the finest quality, and when in a bind, you need to trust that you have what you need. If this is Players Light rather than fair trade organic, that's okay. The Metis medicine man I worked with who shared his tobacco teachings with me was always clear that it is what's in your heart that matters. Bless you, Greg Calliou.

Acknowledgments

I begin with the ancestors—in particular, my mother's spirit—who have driven me to listen and complete this body of work. May I continue to heed your call. May this book find its way into the hands of those who need it.

I give thanks to all my early manuscript readers through the years: Maren, Fairy Godmother Victoria, Avalon, Aviva, Edith, Teresa, Marlene, Gael and Annette, your feedback through stages and ages was invaluable. Those of you in the First Readers Group who read it all, offered testimonials and took time to pin-point what was poignant and powerful – Thank you. There are also many of you whom listened to snippets, read bits and held space for this process. Every single one of you has midwifed this creation.

My editors—Mary Beth Conlee, who went through the gregarious work of supporting me from one idea to the other over the course of twelve months, bringing much-needed structure to my vision—and Christine Savage, whose proofreading and finesse added to the final touches.

Friesen Press, gratitude for the systems you have in place that have guided me in the journey from writer to author, making this dream a reality.

For my sister Kirsten, just because.

To my students, program participants and private session clients over the past decade: your ability to bare your soul and go into the underworld with me has deepened my faith and resolution with this work. Thank you.

Thank you to my immediate family: Mark, Johanna, Hayley, William, Jessica, and Merissa, for all your love and understanding of the space I had to step into as I worked on this through the years.

And most importantly, I thank you, the reader, for taking the time to read my story.

Permissions

Quotes are used with permission or in accordance with standard copyright law, and individual publishing companies policies, they are accredited in alphabetical order by author

- Brené Brown's quote from *Gifts of Imperfection* and all other Brené Brown quotes are used in accordance with her policy at https://brenebrown.com/faq/.
- Quote from Wayne Dyer found online May 2020
- Excerpt from WOMEN WHO RUN WITH THE WOLVES by Clarissa Pinkola Estes, Ph.D., copyright © 1992, 1995 by Clarissa Pinkola Estes, Ph.D., Used with permission of Ballantine Books, an imprint of Random House, a division of Penguin Random House LLC. All rights reserved.
- Excerpt from *Man's Search for Meaning* by Viktor E. Frankl, published by Beacon Press, copyright © 1959 by Victor E. Frankl. Reprinted with permission from the publisher.
- From the book *Creative Visualization*. Copyright ©2002 by Shakti Gawain. Reprinted with permission of New World Library, Novato, CA. www.newworldlibrary.com.
- Excerpt from Together we are One, by Thich Nhat Hanh, copyright © 2010 Unified Buddhist Church.
- Excerpt from *Waking the Tiger: Healing Trauma* by Peter A. Levine, published by North Atlantic Books, copyright © 1997 by Peter A. Levine. Reprinted by permission of publisher.
- Quote from My Grandmothers Hands, by Resmaa Manakem found online June 2020 at resmaa.com, reprinted in alignment with publisher's regulations on quotes.

- Excerpt from *In the Realm of the Hungry Ghosts, Close Encounters with Addiction,* by Gabor Mate, published by Vintage Canada, copyright © 2008 by Gabor Mate, used with permission from the Author.
- Quote from *Trauma not Transformed is Trauma Transferred,* Tabitha Mpamira-Kagur, used with her permission. See her TED talk at https://www.youtube.com/watch?v=b4loBphYCXI.
- Excerpt from *Alchemical Healing, A Guide To Spiritual, Physical And Transformational Medicine,* by Nicki Scully, published by Bear and Co, copyright ©2003 by Nicki Scully, used with permission from the Author.
- Excerpts from *Wild Mercy, Living the Fierce and Tender Wisdom of the Women Mystics,* by Mirabai Starr, published by Sounds True, copyright © 2019 by Mirabai Starr, used with permission from the Author.
- Excerpt from GRANDMOTHERS COUNSEL THE WORLD, by Carol Schaefer, quote from Grandmother Clara, © 2006 by Carol Schaefer, Reprinted by arrangement with Shambhala Publications, Inc., Boulder, CO. www.shambhala.com
- Excerpt from *The Book of Forgiving,* by Desmond M. Tutu and Mpho A. Tutu, copyright © 2014 by Desmond M. Tutu and Mpho A. Tutu. Used by permission of Harper Collins Publishers.
- Excerpt from *THE BODY KEEPS THE SCORE: BRAIN, MIND, AND BODY IN THE HEALING OF TRAUMA,* by Bessel van der Kolk, © 2014 by Bessel van der Kolk, used by permission of Viking Books, an imprint of Penguin publishing Group, a division of Penguin Random House LLC. All rights reserved.

Resources, References and Next Steps

The number of books or videos one might choose to explore the topics in this book are endless. In as much I have created a resource page on my website, updated regularly to support your journey of discovery, healing and education.

Go to www.sarahsalterkelly.com

What are your next steps to put *Trauma as Medicine* into practice?
- Purchase pre-recorded shamanic journeys, guided meditations and exercises from my website to compliment your healing
- Join the *Trauma as Medicine* Facebook page to engage in conversations
- Sign up for an online *Trauma as Medicine* course, mentored by myself
- Join me for an in person *Trauma as Medicine* retreat
- Book a private session with me
- Follow me on Instagram @sarahsalterkelly
- Send me a note info@sarahsalterkelly.com

Find information on all the above at www.sarahsalterkelly.com.

Invite me to speak at your conference and/or teach a *Trauma as Medicine* workshop for your group

"Out of the darkest of tragedies, Sarah shares her own story of healing and reconciliation through her powerful talks and workshops, inspiring and motivating others to take the steps towards their own healing path."

–**Sue Hopgood,** Consulting Ltd. Engage-RP.com

Invite Marilyn and I to share our stories for your organization

"Sarah and Marilyn, you have such tremendous gifts as speakers and teachers.

The feedback we've received from your talk has been incredible. I feel like everyone walked out of the event a little more human. I know your stories and wisdom have been hard-won, so thank you for sharing them with all of us."

–**Jared Tkachuk,** Manager, Outreach and Support Services, Boyle Street Community Services

Please contact me directly at info@sarahsalterkelly.com, at 1-780-314-9150, or go to www.sarahsalterkelly.com.

Ordering in Bulk: If you are working in a human service field, such as therapists, psychologists, social work, victim services, or restorative justice, and are interested in sharing *Trauma as Medicine* with your organization, contact me to get a discount for your bulk purchase.

About the Author

Sarah Salter Kelly wonders the wilds of Western Canada with the love of her life - Mark Kelly and occasional near grown children in tow, exploring natures beauty through a daily practice of connection.

She is a skilled ceremonialist, healer and teacher who sometimes forays into civilization for public speaking, teaching retreats, or to offer in person courses and events.

Her teachings in spiritual healing are rooted in the awareness that we are not separate from our suffering and in as much need to form a relationship with our grief and trauma to allow it to do the work it is intended for - crack us upon and awaken us to truth.

For twenty-five years Sarah has learned to embody her philosophies by addressing the trauma of her mothers brutal kidnapping and homicide, forgiving the perpetrator, and putting together trauma focussed workshops to help others.

Trauma as Medicine is the result of this soul intensive labour, birthing a guideline infused with love, stories, and teachings to support readers far and wide in tending to their greatest suffering. It is based solely on lived experience, combining resources and tools necessary to give the reader confidence in their ability to heal themselves.

Her passion for writing began with poetry, song writing and journaling from the time she could hold a pen. This is her first book. She is certain it is not the last.

Printed in Canada